UNITED NATIONS CONFERENCE
Ger

MW00761495

ECONOMIC DEVELOPMENT
IN AFRICA

Rethinking the Role of
Foreign Direct Investment

UNITED NATIONS
New York and Geneva, 2005

NOTE

Symbols of United Nations documents are composed of capital letters combined with figures. Mention of such a symbol indicates a reference to a United Nations document.

The designations employed and the presentation of the material in this publication do not imply the expression of any opinion whatsoever on the part of the Secretariat of the United Nations concerning the legal status of any country, territory, city or area, or of its authorities, or concerning the delimitation of its frontiers or boundaries.

Material in this publication may be freely quoted or reprinted, but acknowledgement is requested, together with a reference to the document number. A copy of the publication containing the quotation or reprint should be sent to the UNCTAD secretariat.

UNCTAD/GDS/AFRICA/2005/1

UNITED NATIONS PUBLICATION
Sales No. E.05.II.D.12
ISBN 92-1-112671-1

CONTENTS

List of Boxes

List of Figures

List of Tables

List of Appendix Tables

Explanatory Notes

The $ sign refers to the US dollar.

Sub-Saharan Africa (SSA): Except where otherwise stated, this includes South Africa.

North Africa: Unlike in the UNCTAD *Handbook of Statistics*, in this publication Sudan is classified as part of sub-Saharan Africa, not North Africa.

Abbreviations

ACP	African, Caribbean and Pacific (group of States)
AEC	African Economic Community
AGOA	African Growth and Opportunity Act
AU	African Union
BCEAO	Banque Centrale des Etats de l'Afrique de l'Ouest
BEAC	Banque des Etats de l'Afrique Centrale
CEN-SAD	Community of Sahel-Saharan States
CEPR	Centre for Economic Policy Research
CODELCO	National Copper Corporation (Chile)
COMESA	Common Market for Eastern and Southern Africa
DBSA	Development Bank of South Africa
DFID	Department for International Development (UK)
ECA	Economic Commission for Africa
ECCAS	Economic Community of Central African States
ECLAC	Economic Commission for Latin America and the Caribbean
ECOWAS	Economic Community of West African States
EIR	Extractive Industries Review
EPA	Economic Partnership Agreement
EPZ	export processing zone
EU	European Union
FAO	Food and Agriculture Organization
FDI	foreign direct investment
FTA	Free Trade Area
GATT	General Agreement on Tariffs and Trade
GATS	General Agreement on Trade in Services
GDP	gross domestic product
GFCF	gross fixed capital formation
GNP	gross national product
G24	Intergovernmental Group of Twenty-Four on International Monetary Affairs
ICSID	International Center for Settlement of Investment Disputes
IDC	Industrial Development Corporation
IFC	International Finance Corporation
IFI	international finance institution

IGAD	Inter-Governmental Authority on Development
ILO	International Labour Organization
IMF	International Monetary Fund
IMF-BOP	International Monetary Fund – Balance of Payment
ITRS	International Transactions Reporting System
LDCs	least developed countries
M&As	mergers and acquisitions
MDGs	Millennium Development Goals
MFA	Multi-Fibre Arrangement
MIGA	Multilateral Investment Guarantee Agency
MVA	manufacturing value added
NEPAD	New Partnership for Africa's Development
NGO	non-governmental organization
NIE	newly-industrialized economy
ODA	official development assistance
OECD	Organisation for Economic Co-operation and Development
PRSP	Poverty Reduction Strategy Paper
R&D	research and development
RTA	regional trading arrangement
SADC	Southern African Development Community
SACU	Southern African Customs Union
SOE	state-owned enterprise
SSA	sub-Saharan Africa
TNC	transnational corporation
TRIMs	trade-related investment measures
TRIPs	trade-related aspects of intellectual property rights
UK	United Kingdom
UMA	Arab Maghreb Union
UNECE	United Nations Economic Commission for Europe
UNIDO	United Nations Industrial Development Organization
UNU	United Nations University
US	United States of America
VAT	value added tax
WBG	World Bank Group
WTO	World Trade Organization

A. Introduction

In the face of inadequate resources to finance long-term development in Africa and with poverty reduction and other Millennium Development Goals (MDGs) looking increasingly difficult to achieve by 2015, attracting foreign direct investment (FDI) has assumed a prominent place in the strategies of economic renewal being advocated by policy makers at the national, regional and international levels. The experience of a small number of fast-growing East Asian newly industrialized economies (NIEs), and recently China, has strengthened the belief that attracting FDI is key to bridging the resource gap of low-income countries and avoiding further build-up of debt while directly tackling the causes of poverty. Since the Asian crisis, while on the one hand a more cautionary note has been sounded about premature financial liberalization, on the other hand calls for an accelerated pace of opening up to FDI have intensified, on the assumption that this will bring not only more stable capital inflows but also greater technological know-how, higher-paying jobs, entrepreneurial and workplace skills, and new export opportunities (Prasad et al., 2003).

This is not an altogether new direction in development policy thinking, particularly in the African context. Immediately following independence, policy makers across the region hoped that attracting FDI, often with the bait of high tariff protection and generous incentive packages, would provide the catalyst for a "late industrialization" drive (Mkandawire, 2001: 306). And following the debt crisis of the early 1980s, the architects of structural adjustment also saw increased FDI as key to sustained economic recovery, this time in conformity with "market fundamentals". From this perspective, the pursuit of responsible macroeconomic policies combined with an accelerating pace of liberalization, deregulation and, above all, privatization were expected to attract FDI to Africa (World Bank, 1997: 51; IMF, 1999).

Despite the efforts of African governments to comply with this policy advice, the record of the past two decades with respect to reducing poverty and attracting FDI has been disappointing at best. In response, a second generation of reforms, introduced in the late 1990s, has sought to address shortcomings in programme design and implementation by placing much greater emphasis on poverty reduction, combined with policy ownership, credibility and transparency. Here too, the promise of getting governance right has been greater flows of FDI, which, along with related measures to improve the investment climate, are expected to spur economic growth and thereby reduce poverty. In this latest attempt to forge consensus on African development, the contrast between relatively high returns on FDI in Africa and the persistently low level of actual flows is seen as not only indicative of past policy mistakes but also suggestive of the potential rewards awaiting the region if it can improve its governance image in the eyes of international business (World Bank, 2002: 102; Collier and Patillo, 1999). In this vein, a recent report by the OECD (2002: 8) attributes the "spectacular failure" of African countries to attract FDI to a mix of unsustainable national economic policies, poor-quality services, closed trade regimes, and problems of political legitimacy, thus advising governments to redesign their macroeconomic, trade and industrial policies to attract FDI. Recent surges of FDI to some countries have been taken as a sign that opening Africa up to international business can bring about a rapid and region-wide "economic renaissance".[1]

This year's report proceeds from the need to take a more critical approach to evaluating the size and impact of FDI in African countries. Building on past years' reports, it first suggests that the exclusive emphasis on market-oriented reform and governance as determinants of the size of FDI flows to Africa is misleading. Once it is recognized that in most countries these flows tend to be more a lagging than a leading factor in the growth and development process, the role of FDI in Africa cannot be properly assessed independently of the disappointing record of reform programmes with respect to growth, capital accumulation and economic diversification. Indeed, while these programmes have been designed and promoted with the aim, *inter alia*, of attracting foreign investors, this record goes much further in explaining the region's FDI performance than the governance failures routinely compiled to describe Africa's poor investment climate.

Secondly, the report argues that FDI carries costs as well as benefits for the host country; consequently, policy makers must fully evaluate the impact of FDI if it is to become a complementary component of a wider package of development measures needed to raise growth, create jobs and diversify into more dynamic activities. Any such evaluation needs to take account of structural biases in African economies, including their longstanding dependence on commodity exports as well as a deindustrialization trend following the debt crisis of the early 1980s. The report suggests that failure to design policies with these challenges in mind runs the danger of recreating a pattern of FDI-led enclave development even if, as has recently been the case in the mining sector, FDI begins to flow to the region on a larger scale. Indeed, while programmes designed to deregulate the mining sector can claim some success in attracting FDI in recent years, a positive developmental impact has failed to materialize. Accordingly, the report calls for a rethinking of the one-sided emphasis on attracting FDI and its replacement with a more balanced and more strategic approach tailored to African economic conditions and development challenges.

B. FDI to Africa: facts and fables

1. Some stylized facts

The volume of flows to Africa is very low compared to flows to other developing regions...

Average annual FDI flows to Africa doubled during the 1980s to $2.2 billion compared to the 1970s, but increased significantly to $6.2 billion and $13.8 billion respectively during the 1990s and 2000–2003. On a per capita basis, this translates into a more than fourfold increase compared to the 1980s. Nevertheless, a casual comparison of these figures with flows to other developing regions is likely to give rise to a simple story about Africa's marginalization in today's increasingly globalizing world: Africa receives a very low share of total global flows and flows to developing countries, and both have been on a steady downward trend for three decades (table 1); the continent now accounts for just 2 to 3 per cent of global flows, down from a peak of 6 per cent in the mid-1970s, and for less than 9 per cent of developing-country flows compared to an earlier peak of 28 per cent in 1976. Stock figures (though less reliable) show a similar picture; indeed, the descent is perhaps even more precipitous given that Africa ended the 1960s with a relatively large stock of FDI in comparison to most other developing regions (Dunning, 1984, table 5.2). Even on a per capita basis, the gap between Africa and other developing regions widened significantly in the 1990s and remains very large despite a recent narrowing (table 1).

A corollary of these trends is that, in contrast with all other developing regions, Africa has remained aid-dependent, with FDI generally lagging behind official development assistance (ODA); between 1970 and 2003, FDI accounted for just one-fifth of all capital flows to Africa. That lag is evident in sub-Saharan Africa (SSA). In North Africa and a few SSA countries, FDI has also trailed labour remittances as a source of foreign savings (although this trend appears to have been reversed in recent years). However, since the early 1990s — when Africa experienced a "lost decade" in terms of declining aid flows — the share of FDI has risen sharply averaging roughly one-third of total capital inflows to Africa during 2000–2003.

Table 1

FDI INFLOWS AND SHARES TO DEVELOPING REGIONS, 1970–2003

(Millions of dollars)

	Average for period			2000	2001	2002	2003
	1970–1979	1980–1989	1990–1999				
World	24 124	93 887	401 028	1 387 953	817 574	678 751	560 115
Developing countries	6 109	21 356	121 769	252 459	219 721	157 612	172 033
Africa	1066	2 162	6 187	8 728	19 616	11 780	15 033
North Africa	160	889	1 864	2 525	4 916	2 918	4 434
Sub-Saharan Africa (SSA)	906	1 273	4 323	6 202	14 700	8 862	10 599
SSA less South Africa	813	1 259	3 472	5 314	7 911	8 105	9 836
Latin America and the Caribbean	3 269	7 438	44 432	97 537	88 139	51 358	49 722
Asia and the Pacific	1 774	11 756	71 150	146 195	111 966	94 474	107 278
Share of country groups in world (%)							
Developing countries	25.3	22.7	30.4	18.2	26.9	23.2	30.7
Africa	4.4	2.3	1.5	0.6	2.4	1.7	2.7
North Africa	0.7	0.9	0.5	0.2	0.6	0.4	0.8
Sub-Saharan Africa	3.8	1.4	1.1	0.4	1.8	1.3	1.9
SSA less South Africa	3.4	1.3	0.9	0.4	1.0	1.2	1.8
Latin America and the Caribbean	13.6	7.9	11.1	7.0	10.8	7.6	8.9
Asia and the Pacific	7.4	12.5	17.7	10.5	13.7	13.9	19.2
Share in total developing countries (%)							
Africa	17.4	10.1	5.1	3.5	8.9	7.5	8.7
North Africa	2.6	4.2	1.5	1.0	2.2	1.9	2.6
Sub-Saharan Africa	14.8	6.0	3.5	2.5	6.7	5.6	6.2
SSA less South Africa	13.3	5.9	2.9	2.1	3.6	5.1	5.7
Latin America and the Caribbean	53.5	34.8	36.5	38.6	40.1	32.6	28.9
Asia and the Pacific	29.0	55.0	58.4	57.9	51.0	59.9	62.4
FDI inflows per capita (dollars)							
Africa	2.6	4.0	8.8	11.0	24.1	14.2	17.7
North Africa	2.1	8.9	14.9	18.3	35.1	20.5	30.6
Sub-Saharan Africa	2.8	2.9	7.5	9.4	21.8	12.8	15.0
SSA less South Africa	2.7	3.1	6.5	8.6	12.6	12.6	14.9
Latin America and the Caribbean	10.4	18.9	94.5	190.7	169.9	97.6	93.1
Asia and the Pacific	0.7	4.2	21.7	41.4	31.3	26.1	29.2
Memo item: Africa's share of global FDI inflows to its share of global income	1.39	0.81	0.86	-	-	-	-

Source: UNCTAD secretariat computations based on UNCTAD FDI/TNC database and World Bank online data.

...but not to its economic weight in the global economy or local economic dynamics.

A comparison across regions offers only a partial perspective on FDI trends and can be misleading if not properly situated in a broader economic context. Over the past three decades, Africa's share of world output has also been declining, dropping decade by decade from 3.1 per cent in the 1970s to 1.8 per cent in the period 2000–2003. Africa's share of world trade also fell over this period from a peak of around 6 per cent in 1980 to around 2 per cent in 2001 before recovering slightly to 2.2 per cent in 2004. More significantly, income levels have stagnated: in per capita terms these are lower for the region as a whole, and for most countries, than they were in 1980. Matched against this performance, the scale of FDI to Africa hardly appears surprising, and it is perhaps just as appropriate to ask how Africa has been able to attract so much FDI as to ask why it has attracted so little; in fact, the ratio of Africa's share in global FDI flows to its share in global output has remained broadly unchanged over this period. Over the same period, the share of gross fixed capital formation in GDP has also dropped persistently on a decade-by-decade basis, notably so in SSA, where the fall was from close to 25 per cent in the late 1970s to 17.2 per cent in the late 1990s (UNCTAD, 2003a: 67), with a further decline in the opening years of the new century. Indeed, and like elsewhere, FDI as a share of gross capital formation has actually been rising in Africa, particularly starting in the mid-1990s; since the turn of the century, it has become a more prominent source of capital formation than in any developing region other than Central Asia.

Geography matters in shaping these flows...

Much has been made of Africa's unfavourable geography, including its distance from leading markets, the number of land-locked countries, low population density and unfavourable climatic conditions. However, and without denying the potentially damaging effects these factors can have on wider development prospects, at least with respect to FDI flows, their significance can be easily exaggerated, particularly in comparison to other developing regions.[2] Certainly geographical distance cannot by itself explain why Latin America is a larger recipient of FDI from Western Europe, nor does land-locked status appear to have been an extra obstacle to attracting FDI in countries such as Chad, Swaziland and Uganda, which are among the region's largest recipients of FDI relative to their economic size. Indeed, taking the group of African land-locked countries together, their share of FDI in GDP between 1985 and 2003 has on average been somewhat higher than for the rest of the region (figure 1).

Geography has bequeathed the continent an impressive endowment of mineral wealth, including near-global monopolies of platinum, chromium and diamonds; a high proportion of the world's gold, cobalt and manganese reserves; and extensive reserves of bauxite, coal, uranium, copper and nickel.

Figure 1

FDI INWARD STOCKS OF AFRICAN LANDLOCKED COUNTRIES
COMPARED TO OTHER AFRICA, 1985 AND 2003

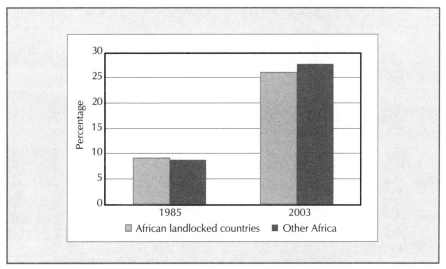

Source: UNCTAD secretariat computations based on UNCTAD FDI/TNC database.

Note: Other Africa does not include South Africa.

North Africa, Nigeria and Gabon have long been major producers of oil, and more recently Angola, Chad, Equatorial Guinea and Sudan have emerged, or re-emerged, as important suppliers; indeed, oil reserves on the continent are by some estimates higher than those of any other region outside the Middle East.

The attraction of Africa's natural resources accounts for the uneven spread of FDI flows across the continent. The 24 countries in Africa classified by the World Bank as oil- and mineral-dependent have on average accounted for close to three-quarters of annual FDI flows over the past two decades, and, with the exception of Mauritius, Morocco and Uganda, which featured among the top 10 recipients in some years during 1999–2003, all the countries in table 2 have large natural resource endowments. Indeed, with the discovery of new oil fields in Chad and Equatorial Guinea, all top 10 recipients of FDI in Africa in 2003 have large mineral and petroleum reserves. Consequently, FDI flows to Africa are very heavily concentrated, with the top 10 recipients consistently accounting for three-quarters or more of the total FDI inflows to the continent; and, although direct comparisons should again be drawn with caution, this is along the lines seen elsewhere (table 2).

Table 2

DEVELOPING-COUNTRY GROUPS: TOP 5 AND TOP 10 RECIPIENTS OF FDI, 1999–2003

Million dollars

	1999		2000		2001		2002		2003		Memo item: Population share at 2001
	Country/Region	Value	Country/Region	Value	Country/Region	Value	Country/Region	Value	Country/Region	Value	Value
	Angola	2471	Egypt	1235	South Africa	6789	Angola	1643	Morocco	2279	–
	South Africa	1502	Nigeria	930	Morocco	2825	Nigeria	1281	Equat. Guinea	1431	–
	Egypt	1065	South Africa	888	Angola	2146	Algeria	1065	Angola	1415	–
	Nigeria	1005	Angola	879	Algeria	1196	Chad	1030	Sudan	1349	–
	Morocco	850	Tunisia	779	Nigeria	1104	Tunisia	821	Nigeria	1200	–
	Tanzania	542	Algeria	438	Equat. Guinea	931	South Africa	757	Chad	837	–
	Algeria	507	Sudan	392	Sudan	574	Sudan	713	South Africa	762	–
	Congo	491	Tanzania	282	Egypt	510	Egypt	647	Libya	700	–
	Mozambique	382	Mauritius	277	Tunisia	486	Morocco	481	Algeria	634	–
	Sudan	371	Uganda	275	Tanzania	467	Botswana	405	Tunisia	584	–
	Per cent		**Per cent**		**Per cent**		**Per cent**		**Per cent**		**Per cent**
	Top 5 to Africa	**59.5**	Top 5 to Africa	**54.0**	Top 5 to Africa	**71.7**	Top 5 to Africa	**49.6**	Top 5 to Africa	**51.0**	30.4
	Top 10 to Africa	**79.3**	Top 10 to Africa	**73.0**	Top 10 to Africa	**86.8**	Top 10 to Africa	**75.1**	Top 10 to Africa	**74.4**	47.8
	Top 5 to dev'g America	**88.3**	Top 5 to dev'g America	**87.6**	Top 5 to dev'g America	**84.9**	Top 5 to dev'g America	**81.5**	Top 5 to dev'g America	**77.9**	68.5
	Top10 to dev'g America	**95.6**	Top10 to dev'g America	**94.8**	Top10 to dev'g America	**94.3**	Top10 to dev'g America	**92.0**	Top10 to dev'g America	**91.5**	84.8
	Top 5 to dev'g Asia	**87.1**	Top 5 to dev'g Asia	**91.7**	Top 5 to dev'g Asia	**84.7**	Top 5 to dev'g Asia	**82.2**	Top 5 to dev'g Asia	**81.9**	68.7
	Top 10 to dev'g Asia	**97.7**	Top 10 to dev'g Asia	**102.5**	Top 10 to dev'g Asia	**97.8**	Top 10 to dev'g Asia	**90.9**	Top 10 to dev'g Asia	**92.5**	75.6

Source: UNCTAD secretariat computations based on UNCTAD FDI/TNC database and World Bank online data.

Notes: * Bermuda, Cayman Islands and Virgin Islands (British) are not included in computations of Latin America and the Caribbean.

         ** Hong Kong (China) and Singapore are not included in computations of developing Asia.

..but history also matters, and perhaps even more so...

One prominent legacy of Africa's colonial history is the predominance of small countries; 31 countries have a population of 10 million or less, and most of these less than 5 million. Given the importance of market size in attracting FDI, this is a potentially significant constraint on inflows to the region. Just as importantly, Africa's insertion into the international division of labour was driven by a pattern of trade between rich country markets and nationals of rich countries producing abroad, whether in firms or farms. A lasting legacy of that history is the region's dependence on a small number of home countries for FDI. Between 1980 and 2000, just three countries, France and the United Kingdom (the two leading former colonial powers) and the United States, accounted for close to 70 per cent of total flows to the continent, and until 1995 the first two accounted for well over 50 per cent of those flows (UNCTAD, 2002a: 51).[3] While regional comparisons are hindered by missing data, a breakdown of stock figures for 2002 suggests a significantly higher concentration in Africa of investors from its three leading home countries than is the case in Latin America, in South, East and South-East Asia, and in Central and Eastern Europe (UNCTAD, 2005a, table 3). Also related to this history is the small scale of intra-regional FDI — only 3 per cent of the FDI stock in Africa originated from the continent itself, compared to close to 30 per cent in South, East and South-East Asia — and confined mainly to the Southern African Development Community (SADC) region; although the re-emergence of South Africa as a home country is beginning to alter this pattern (box 1).

...with consequences for the structural composition of FDI flows...

A distinct feature of FDI flows to Africa is their sectoral bias. While data here are difficult to find on a continuous basis and often draw on a restricted sample of countries, the picture of flows heavily concentrated in primary activities is not disputed (Cantwell, 1997). A breakdown of stock figures for 1988 and 1997 shows a slight increase in the primary share from 51.8 per cent to 53.4 per cent of the total stock in Africa, compared to a decline in Asia from 8.8 per cent to 3.5 per cent and in Latin America from 8.8 to 5.7 per cent (UNCTAD, 1999a: 424–425). Flows between 1996 and 2000 continued to be concentrated in the primary sector, accounting for nearly 55 per cent of total flows to Africa from major investors, but reaching as high as 80 per cent in some years (UNCTAD, 2002a: 52). By way of comparison, between 1990 and 2002 the share of the primary sector in the total stock of FDI in developing countries showed little change, rising marginally from 6.7 per cent to 7 per cent.

Box 1

SOUTH AFRICA'S EXPANDING INVESTMENT IN AFRICA

The South African economy is the largest in Africa: it contributes about 20 per cent of the continent's GDP and roughly one-third and two-thirds respectively of the total output of sub-Saharan Africa and the SADC region. South Africa's exports to the rest of Africa have grown phenomenally over the past decade and a half and currently exceed those to the United States and the European Union, typically accounting for about 15 to 20 per cent of total exports. This has been accompanied by an expansion of South African companies to the rest of the continent in the areas of mining, civil engineering and construction, agriculture, tourism and hotels, and manufacturing and services, including transport and telecommunications; and recently in the oil and gas sectors, mostly in West Africa. Some African countries have also hosted South African investments in the commercial and retail sectors.

The country was the largest investor into the rest of the continent during the period 1990 to 2000, with investments averaging about $1.4 billion yearly, or a total of about $12.5 billion over the decade. Much of this investment was in the second half of the 1990s and was concentrated in neighbouring countries. In a recent survey, only one non-SADC country, Kenya, featured in the top destinations; non-SACU investment is dominated by Zambia and Zimbabwe, both of which have a strong mining heritage. The fact that South African companies made more new investments in Africa in the last three years than in the five years to 2000 suggests that these cross-border investments have yet to peak. The new investments are concentrated in minerals and energy and, since 2001, include newer countries such as Algeria, Burkina Faso, Equatorial Guinea, Gabon, Mauritania, Morocco and Sao Tome and Principe.

South African parastatal organizations have also participated in South Africa's cross-border investment activities. Financial parastatals such as the Industrial Development Corporation (IDC) and the Development Bank of South Africa (DBSA) have provided finance to a variety of sectors and acted as levers for South African and international investment in host countries, the most prominent example of which is the Mozal smelter in Mozambique. Spoornet (a state rail operator) operates or manages rail networks in 14 countries across the continent, while Eskom (a power utility) through its commercial arm, Eskom Enterprises, is an important player in the development of the electrical power sector in SADC and, to a limited extent, outside SADC as well.

Source: South Africa Foundation, June 2004.

... the kind of profit-investment nexus established by these flows...

Africa's particular combination of geographical, historical and structural features have traditionally attracted FDI in to enclaves of export-oriented primary production using a good deal of imported technology and with limited linkages to the rest of the economy. In the absence of national input-output tables, the significance of enclave production can be indirectly gauged by a country's GDP (a measure of the value of output generated within national boundaries) being much higher than its GNP (a measure of the income actually earned by national citizens), by a high ratio of export earnings to value added, and by the presence of a large informal economy (Todaro, 1983: 357). Such economies also tend to exhibit periodic profit surges, often well in excess of FDI inflows. These features of enclavism still appear to characterize many African countries and may have intensified over the past two decades (appendix tables). Significantly, reinvested profits are also a less important source of FDI for Africa than for other regions, despite the very high returns on investment. Between 1995 and 2002, equity FDI accounted for about 74 per cent of the total inflows to Africa, similar to the developing-country average, while inter-company loans and reinvested capital accounted for 16 per cent and 10 per cent respectively, compared with 14 and 15 per cent for all developing countries (World Bank, 2004a: 87).

Traditionally, particularly given the capital intensity of the extractive industries, this type of insertion into the global economy has attracted a preponderance of greenfield investments over mergers and acquisitions (M&As). However, in recent years the composition of inflows between these two forms of FDI has shifted towards the latter. M&A transactions increased from an annual average of $0.6 billion in 1990–1994 to over $2.5 billion in 1995–1999 and $7.5 billion in 2000–2003 (16, 30 and 54 per cent of total FDI flows, respectively). These M&As often represent large one-off inflows (although they may trigger subsequent but much smaller flows) and also appear to be very strongly influenced by factors in the home economy (Kamaly, 2003b). They also tend to be heavily concentrated. Overall, South Africa accounts for about half the value of all Africa's M&As between 1990 and 2003, with smaller shares accounted for by Egypt, Morocco and Tunisia. However, in some countries in SSA, such as Ghana, Kenya and Mauritius, M&As have accounted for a very high percentage of inflows in particular years, often as the outcome of privatization programmes.

...and the stability of the investment climate.

There is a general belief that FDI in the oil and mining sectors tends to be more volatile than for other sectors, particularly manufacturing, given the combination of capital-intensive projects and the sensitivity of profits to world commodity prices. (World Bank, 2005a: 97). Moreover, strong growth in these sectors can often assume boom-like conditions, with potentially adverse consequences for investment in other sectors. Certainly during the 1990s, FDI to oil- and mineral-exporting countries in Africa was more volatile than to the rest of the region as a whole (figure 2), and over the last five years (1999–2003) this has contributed to an increase in the volatility of total flows to the region; FDI inflows surged by 30 per cent in 1999 to reach $11.6 billion but then declined 29 per cent to $8.7 billion in 2000. They surged again to $19.6 billion in 2001 but declined sharply again to $11.8 billion in 2002 before recovering to $15 billion in 2003 (table 1). But in addition to large oil and mining projects, these surges are also likely to reflect increased investor interest in the tertiary sector, particularly the privatization of publicly owned service providers. Indeed, there is evidence to suggest these flows are even more volatile than FDI

Figure 2

FDI INFLOWS TO AFRICAN FUEL- AND MINERAL-EXPORTING COUNTRIES
COMPARED TO OTHER AFRICA, 1970 AND 2003

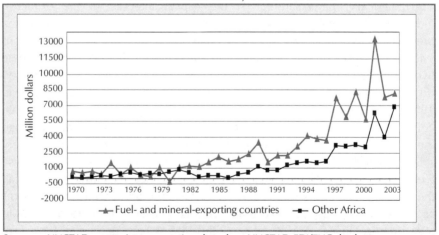

Source: UNCTAD secretariat computations based on UNCTAD FDI/TNC database.
Note: Fuel- and mineral-exporting countries as defined by the World Bank: Algeria, Angola,
            Botswana, Cameroon, Central African Republic, Egypt, Ghana, Guinea, Kenya, Libya,
            Mauritania, Mozambique, Namibia, Niger, Nigeria, Rwanda, Senegal, South Africa,
            Sudan, Togo, Zambia, Zimbabwe.

to the primary sector (UNCTAD, 2002a, table III.3). Still, over the longer term, FDI flows to Africa do not stand out in terms of their volatility, in relation to other developing regions (table 3).

Table 3

VOLATILITY OF FDI INFLOWS, 1970–2003

(Coefficient of variation)

	1970–1979	1980–1989	1990–1999	1994–2003
FDI inflows				
Africa	0.40	0.52	0.52	0.44
North Africa	2.29	0.61	0.37	0.43
Sub-Saharan Africa (SSA)	0.30	0.59	0.63	0.45
Memo item:				
SSA less South Africa	0.40	0.65	0.56	0.41
Asia	1.07	0.48	0.49	0.20
West Asia	7.92	1.56	0.72	0.69
South, East and South-East Asia	0.45	0.59	0.50	0.21
Central Asia	..	..	0.81	0.51
Latin America and the Caribbean	0.47	0.20	0.76	0.40
South America	0.65	0.37	0.86	0.48
Other Latin America and the Caribbean	0.52	0.24	0.62	0.39
FDI inflows as per cent of GDP				
Africa	0.43	0.49	0.46	0.40
North Africa	2.13	0.62	0.31	0.35
Sub-Saharan Africa	0.34	0.51	0.59	0.44
Memo item:				
SSA less South Africa	0.26	0.61	0.52	0.31
Asia	1.01	0.49	0.34	0.16
West Asia	7.81	1.61	0.66	0.80
South, East and South-East Asia	0.23	0.38	0.33	0.19
Central Asia	..	..	0.79	0.42
Latin America and the Caribbean	0.25	0.16	0.64	0.36
South America	0.36	0.32	0.78	0.45
Other Latin America and the Caribbean	0.44	0.35	0.47	0.26

Source: UNCTAD secretariat computations based on UNCTAD FDI/TNC database.

2. Analytical perspectives and methodological caveats

There is clearly a good deal more to evaluating FDI flows in Africa than explaining their comparatively small scale. And while it seems plausible to assume, in light of the economic gaps, weaknesses and distortions typical of less developed regions, that FDI could be playing a more constructive role in African development, identifying when, to what extent and with what effect the profit-making strategies of international firms overlap with the developmental strategies of policy makers is neither a clear nor a simple exercise.

It is generally recognized that the size and distribution of global FDI flows cannot be explained by international capital arbitrage; otherwise, very large flows would be automatically attracted to capital-scarce Africa. Rather, national firms become transnational because they possess specific assets — such as a superior production technology, a distinct product design or managerial and marketing skills — which allow them to undertake profitable investments abroad despite the higher risks and additional costs that arise from coordinating production activities over greater geographical distances and across political borders. By implication, managing those assets within the firm's own hierarchical structure must also be less costly than exploiting them through markets, including via exporting (UNCTAD, 1996a: 76–77). For poorer countries looking to climb the development ladder, gaining access to those same assets raises the prospect of filling various gaps in their own productive structure more rapidly and at lower cost than if they had to rely exclusively on the evolution of their own firms.[4] But given that the additional costs incurred by internationalizing production through FDI tend to be positively correlated with the size of those same gaps, developing countries must also possess some clear advantages that can attract TNCs to their location, whether large markets, abundant natural resources or low wage costs.

Much of the thinking on whether and to what extent corporate and country interests do converge around attracting FDI has centred on how best an eclectic mixing and matching of firm-specific assets and locational advantages can generate large efficiency gains. Such gains essentially hinge on the "internalization" of market failures by TNCs, which simultaneously allows them to deliver an asset "package" to a particular location through FDI that includes not only capital but also productivity enhancing technologies and best corporate norms and practices. Accordingly, and to the extent that there is a degree of "automatic progress" surrounding the unpacking of FDI once local operations are established, the development dimension reduces to the design of appropriate strategies by the host country to attract FDI by abandoning policies that might hinder the establishment of local affiliates and distort the way in which they are integrated into the global operations of the parent company.[5]

However, the promise of automatic efficiency gains from hosting FDI hinges on a number of implicit assumptions. The first is that additions to the capital stock from attracting FDI are "bolted down" in new plant equipment, forcing firms into longer-term commitments and giving policy makers some degree of reciprocal bargaining power once such investments are in place. In reality, FDI can take the form of M&As as well as greenfield investments, and while from a corporate perspective both are additions to productive assets, this is not so for the economy of the host country. Although long-term considerations might play a role in M&As, these can also be greatly influenced by prospects of quick capital gains, particularly during periods of economic crisis (Krugman, 1998). In addition, where finance assumes a more prominent role in shaping international economic relations, liberalization of financial flows and related innovations in financial market instruments allow for hedging of FDI flows and a blurring of the distinction with other types of capital flow. Recognizing that "a firm may be doing one thing with its assets and something quite different with the way it finances them" opens the possibility to a much more "footloose" and less stable type of FDI (Hausmann and Fernandez-Arias, 2000: 8).[6]

A second assumption is that the productive assets bundled into FDI readily spill over to the local economy through competition, imitation, labour turnover or vertical linkages. But in a world where markets fail, scale matters, oligopolistic power is significant, and opaque business practices such as transfer pricing and creative accounting are pervasive, keeping control over specific assets is key to a firm's capacity to generate rents. In such a world, there are plenty of reasons why a one-sided focus on efficiency gains is likely to overestimate the size of positive spillovers from FDI and to underestimate the possible costs, as well as downplaying potential conflicts of interest between TNCs and host governments. Certainly, on balance, and taking account of the different methodologies employed, evidence of positive spillovers from FDI is mixed, but there is little evidence of this in low income developing countries, and virtually none on a significant scale.[7]

A last assumption is that FDI will crowd in domestic investment given the right governance structures, including competitive markets, unrestricted entry and exit of firms, and minimal state intervention. However, it is questionable, particularly in late-industrializing economies, whether governance of the investment process is best left purely to the price mechanism. This is so in part because of information and incentive problems generated by high levels of uncertainty and by externalities and complementarities inherent in that process, but also because rapid capital accumulation depends on the "animal spirits" of domestic entrepreneurs, and competitive markets can often fail to generate profits on a sufficient scale and with the stability that encourages them to commit to the type of longer-term investment projects needed to expand productive capacity, create jobs or build technological depth.[8] Rather, the governance of this process requires various institutional arrangements and interventions by the state to generate, distribute and revoke economic rents and to coordinate investments in a way that meets wider development goals. This implies ongoing interaction and bargaining between policy makers and local entrepreneurs. How this extends to the management of rents created by foreign firms, and their possible impact on the accumulation process, is likely to entail additional challenges for policy makers. Certainly no simple pattern of crowding in or out by FDI emerges from the data (UNCTAD, 2003a: 76–78). Whether or not the rents created by TNCs through FDI add to a local accumulation drive will likely depend on various factors, including corporate strategy set at headquarters; the levels of industrial, technological and skill development reached by local firms, which will have a direct bearing on the viability of any such investment projects; and the bargaining capacities of local state and private actors in the face of the asymmetric market power enjoyed by TNCs.[9]

It follows, in light of these underlying assumptions, that the likely impact of FDI on economic growth and development cannot be derived from the details of corporate strategy but must be viewed in the context of existing domestic economic structures, capacities and strategies. Taking a more prudent view of the FDI package also implies that a high (low) share of FDI in total capital inflows or gross fixed capital formation should not be taken as an unambiguously positive (negative) benchmark of a healthy economic policy environment. Rather, a more balanced framework for evaluating FDI needs to weigh up a series of accompanying costs and benefits, and in relation to a range of development goals, many of which are country- and sector-specific. Adopting such an approach will recognize that the inflow of capital from FDI may be a benefit, but that the subsequent outflow of profits earned on the investment may be so high as to make it a very substantial cost. Again, the production of new foreign subsidiaries may be a benefit, but if it displaces existing production by local firms, this is an offsetting cost. Similarly, extra exports may require higher imports of materials or components. Where the firm does not create new assets, but merely takes over existing locally owned ones, the net benefits may be particularly hard to discern, except perhaps where access to new external markets is opened up (box 2).

In the absence of a balanced framework, the danger persists of substituting a more focussed analysis of the stylized African FDI facts with a "laundry list" of possible determinants of FDI flows to poorer countries. Regression analysis using cross-country, time series and mixed data can provide a semblance of rigour to this compilation exercise by testing which of several possible variables explain the scale and direction of flows. Adopting such an approach will likely be consonant with a wider policy perspective that sees attracting FDI through open markets as part of a bigger process of global economic integration and income convergence.[10]

The limits of this approach with respect to FDI in Africa are reviewed in the next section. However, it is worth noting at the outset that not only is empirical support for the wider convergence thesis inconclusive, but such an approach is also prone to a good deal of terminological and methodological confusion. Concepts such as openness, integration, outward orientation and export promotion are often used interchangeably even though they refer to rather different aspects of international economic relations. More seriously still, they tend to bias the discussion of what constitutes sound development strategy towards "external" economic relations at the expense of "internal integration" and, in particular, a careful analysis of the role of domestic investment and institutions in support of growth.[11] This has led to confusion over the classification of policy measures, interpretive problems over the causal links between policies and economic performance, and a narrowing of policy priorities.[12]

While much of the confusion on the links between openness and economic development has arisen around trade performance and policies, the muddle is even greater with FDI, where methodological snags are compounded by serious data gaps arising from the loose definition of what is being measured, as well as

Box 2

EVALUATING FDI: AN UNCTAD PERSPECTIVE

Conventional approaches to FDI assume that TNCs are the most efficient way of allocating resources on a global scale in the face of international market failures of one kind or another, and that only if left alone from government interference will freely flowing capital act as a powerful force for closing income gaps across the global economy. An alternative view maintains that whether FDI is socially profitable for the host country, and to what extent, is not given a priori on corporate efficiency grounds, but requires careful investigation in the circumstances of each project, and in light of their consistency with development objectives, including income growth and distribution; employment expansion; the absorption of new skills and technology; and balance of payments stability. Profitable investment by a foreign firm may help to achieve some of these objectives, but may hamper the achievement of others. In designing policies to meet these objectives, the possibility of divergent interests between company and country forms the backdrop for possible options. Because neither the costs nor the benefits will be instantaneous, policy design will be complicated by the sequencing of complementary measures as projects progress. Attention must also be given to the economy after the projects have been chosen, taking into account not just the impact of these projects but the situation that would prevail in their absence, as well as to alternative sources of delivery, whether through joint ventures, production by domestic firms, importing and other market channels, or doing without. Evaluation will also need to take into account the type of good being produced, whether luxury, mass consumption, intermediate or capital goods, as well as the appropriateness of production techniques for local conditions.

Neither theory nor history suggests that economic catch-up can be left to the interplay of global market forces and large international firms from advanced industrial countries. In fact, while domestic firms in poorer countries might have some advantage over TNCs in terms of local knowledge and contacts, they are likely to face significant disadvantages in terms of access to capital, foreign markets and technology and in terms of skill levels and their intellectual property. Thus a persistent problem for developing countries is to what extent they can secure the benefits from hosting TNCs without becoming dominated by them or permitting their economic development to be distorted. And at a fundamental level, policy towards FDI will ultimately depend not just on clear and direct evidence of positive spillovers but on evidence that domestic firms are in a position to benefit. This will involve policy makers in gathering appropriate data, monitoring of and bargaining with foreign investors, and judging whether and at what pace activities might become owned and controlled by local firms. In this respect, policy making towards FDI is best seen as part of a discovery process where firms and government learn about profit opportunities and their underlying cost structure; where creating, monitoring and withdrawing rents are key to generating a more diversified economic profile; and where coordination strategies are needed to manage large and complementary investment projects that help realize scale economies.

Sources: Sen, 1971; UNCTAD, 1972; UNCTAD, 1997; Hanson, 2001.

collection and coverage problems. The standard definition of FDI as a "long-term" relationship involving a "significant degree of influence" on the management of the enterprise encompasses a heterogeneous group of corporate actors, some with complex integrated production structures, others with little more than a sales outlet in a single foreign market, a problem that is hardly resolved by reducing the control threshold to a minimum 10 per cent equity claim. Such fundamental definitional problems are aggravated by the fact that aggregate FDI flows are a composite of different sources including equity flows from abroad, undistributed profits and inter-company loans. Clearly, some of these flows do not involve cross-border transactions, and their treatment as a one-way inflow item in the capital account complicates statistical measurement as well as evaluation of its impact (UNCTAD, 1999b: 117).[13] And although the conceptual distinction between M&As and greenfield investment is reasonably straightforward in theory, it is much more difficult to apply to available statistics (UNCTAD, 2000a: 105–106). While these problems accompany the study of FDI generally, they are exaggerated in the African context, where data gaps and paucity are particularly pronounced (box 3).

Box 3

FDI DATA: HARMONIZED APPROACH IS VITAL FOR POLICY ANALYSIS

Data gathering and accounting procedures, legal constraints, confidentiality concerns and lack of trained personnel hamper the collection and compilation of FDI data in most developing countries. Stock estimates and the breakdown of sources of FDI are at best based on (irregular) survey data, and data on M&As is particularly problematic, with multiple definition and collection problems complicating the use of the available figures. In addition, corporate practices such as "transfer pricing" and "round tripping" complicate data compilation. According to the IMF (2004: 10), between 1996 and 2002 some two dozen countries, mostly in Africa, fell behind in reporting their balance of payments statistics, and even where current data do exist, comparability is often made difficult by the use of different definitions and methods of FDI data collection, and because accounting practices and valuation methods for FDI data differ among countries. A large number of African countries do not appear to have an explicit definition of FDI at all, and this, coupled with capacity constraints, makes it likely that only a fraction of what constitutes FDI by the internationally adopted standard definition is actually accounted for in the data that the national authorities report in their balance-of-payments account. In seven African countries (Lesotho, Mauritius, Namibia, Seychelles, Sierra Leone, South Africa and Togo) FDI is defined in accordance with the ITRS (International Transactions

---

Box 3 (contd.)

Reporting System) — the International Monetary Fund — Balance of Payment (IMF-BOP) and the Organisation for Economic Co-operation and Development (OECD) manuals. In two groups of countries, one (Benin, Burkina Faso, Côte d'Ivoire, Guinea Bissau, Mali, Niger, Senegal and Togo) belonging to the Banque Centrale des Etats de l'Afrique de l'Ouest (BCEAO) and the other (Cameroon, Central African Republic, Chad, Congo, Equatorial Guinea and Gabon) belonging to the Banque des Etats de l'Afrique Centrale (BEAC), a standard FDI data collection and accounting system has been adopted, but it is not known whether each of the national central banks uses the IMF-BOP manuals. Another 35 African countries did not reflect any clear definition of FDI in the investment codes submitted to the International Centre for Settlement of Investment Disputes (ICSID). Even some larger economies, such as Egypt and Nigeria, do not use methods consistent with the IMF-BOP standard definition. In Egypt, the Information and Decision Support Center reports that the Central Bank collects data through company surveys and does not capture inflows of FDI related to free zones and companies in the petroleum sector. In Nigeria, the Central Bank collects FDI data based on company surveys, but only for companies in which foreigners hold at least 75 per cent of total equity. These approaches deviate significantly from the definition in the IMF-BOP manual, creating a major problem in the accurate measurement and quality of FDI data in the region.

Source: UNCTAD, Divison on Investment, Technology and Enterprise Development.

---

3. FDI flows to Africa:
the limits of conventional wisdom

In line with much conventional development thinking, most recent efforts to understand the determinants of FDI flows to Africa and their impact tend to assume that a rapid pace of opening up is the key to attracting the right type of FDI on the desired scale. From this perspective, Africa's low level of FDI is explained by various "governance failures" that have closed the region off to a new growth dynamic built around participation in international production networks and more efficient service activities.

Problems of policy credibility have been identified as likely deterrents to potential foreign investors, with trade policies singled out for particular attention in cross-country regression studies; low levels of FDI to Africa have been explained by the *ad hoc* and reversible nature of liberalization efforts and the abuse of trade policies for wider economic and social goals (Asiedu, 2002). Others have singled out unfavourable and unstable tax regimes (Gastanaga et al., 1998), the slow pace of public sector reform, particularly privatization, (Akingube, 2003; Pigatto, 2001) and the inadequacy of intellectual property protection (OECD, 2003) as erecting serious obstacles to FDI in Africa. In addition to this perceived policy deficit vis-à-vis other developing regions, excessive levels of corruption, regulation and political risk are believed to have further raised costs, adding to an unattractive "business climate" for FDI (Morrisett, 2000; Elbadawi and Mwega, 1997).

Other studies have stressed macroeconomic policy failures as deflecting FDI flows from the region. According to this assessment, irresponsible fiscal and monetary policies have generated unsustainable budget deficits and inflationary pressures, raising local production costs, generating exchange rate instability, and making the region too risky a location for long-term investments, particularly in more dynamic non-traditional export sectors (Reinhart and Rogoff, 2002; Lyakurwa, 2003). Given a strong correlation between capital account openness and FDI inflows, sluggish financial liberalization has also been identified as adding to Africa's poor macro performance in attracting FDI (Gastanaga et al., 1998; Bende-Nabende, 2002).

These problems of poor policy and weak governance have, in turn, been traced to ingrained anti-colonial and nationalist sentiments, which have allowed obsolete policy thinking to persist longer in Africa than elsewhere (Moss et al., 2004) and rent-seeking coalitions to resist systematic reforms (Basu and Srinivasan, 2002). Others have suggested that reverberations from just a few countries may have tainted the whole region as investor unfriendly (UNCTAD, 1999c). Accordingly, better governance, understood to include increased openness, diminished public-sector control and more transparent and participatory policy procedures, should lower perceptions of risk and strengthen the hand of reformers in implementing adjustment programmes, thereby establishing a more appropriate and predictable incentive structure for attracting foreign investors (Pigatto, 2001).

An immediate shortcoming of these explanations of "governance failure" deflecting FDI from Africa is that they coincide with a period of intensifying adjustment across the region, which has aimed to reduce the role of the state and covers all aspects of monetary and exchange rate policies, financial market reform (including opening up of the capital account), privatization, deregulation, and trade and FDI liberalization. In Africa these policies have been applied more repeatedly and vigorously than in any other region (UNCTAD, 2002b, section C).[14] The fact that these efforts have still not attracted the expected inflows of FDI raises questions about the role of governance reforms, at least as this has been conventionally defined and implemented in Africa.

As has been noted in past UNCTAD reports, a considerable amount of institutional diversity characterizes successful development experiences, including among today's advanced economies, and judging Africa's performance against a narrow and highly stylized standard of what constitutes *good* governance is likely to be misleading and perhaps counterproductive. Certainly, and as was suggested earlier, the successful management of trade in strong growth episodes, including in Africa (see box 7 in section D), has rarely followed a simple or unilinear pattern of accelerating liberalization; and while foreign affiliates, particularly those providing just one link in a longer cross-border value chain, may favour rapid trade liberalization, for developing-country policy makers the trade-investment nexus raises more complex issues, with the likely impact of liberalization on FDI depending on the type of FDI involved, as well as industry and country characteristics (Amiti and Wakelin, 2003). Moreover, and while the identification of a good business climate with weak state institutions and regulations is anyway questionable, a recent comparative study of African competitiveness actually found that, "in terms of business environment (as measured by the World Bank), SSA does not fare badly relative to other developing regions" (Lall, 2004: 22). The countries in SSA have certainly been assiduous in establishing export processing zones (EPZs) — more so than any other developing region outside Asia — and in signing investment treaties (sometimes seen as a measure of good governance), without attracting the expected FDI (Hallward-Driemeier, 2003); and corporate tax rates in Africa do not appear to be at variance with those in other regions (Hanson, 2001: 4). Indeed, a cursory glance at the top of recent league tables of attracting FDI in Africa does not suggest that the responsiveness of TNCs to good political or corporate governance is the driving force behind large inflows.[15]

The extent to which Africa has been more inflation prone than other regions over the past two decades is also debatable (UNCTAD, 2002b). Bosworth and Collins (2003) have ruled this out, along with other macroeconomic price distortions, as a significant explanatory factor in the region's sub-standard growth performance over the past two decades. Findings to the contrary appear to give undue weight to the performance of a small number of conflict-ridden countries, where inflationary pressures have little to do with conventional notions of macroeconomic mismanagement. There also appears to be a tendency to underestimate the extent to which African countries have in practice established more open capital accounts, particularly with respect to FDI, where policy convergence among developing countries has been a strong trend over the past two decades (Ndikumana, 2003; Kobrin, 2005). Moreover, tracing the FDI shortfall to sluggish capital account liberalization ignores how such moves might, by increasing financial volatility, actually deter FDI, particularly where domestic financial markets are weak or missing, as is typically the case in SSA (Hermes and Lensink, 2003; UNCTAD, 1996b), or can attract a type of FDI with less favourable consequences for growth (Lensink and Morrisey, 2002).

The fact that weak, missing or failing markets can deter and distort FDI is not limited to the financial dimension of the package. As was noted above, market failures are a principal reason why TNCs choose to exploit their technological advantages through investments abroad.[16] However, a positive impact from hosting FDI is contingent on the presence of local technological capacities, and while there is no easy blueprint for building a dynamic learning environment in support of technological progress in poorer countries, there is agreement that it will involve a mix of learning on the job along with more formal training and public support, to ensure an adequate supply of skills and know-how with which to absorb, adapt and advance technology, including through attracting and utilizing FDI. Certainly, regarding a series of measures, including formal and vocational training, R&D expenditures and patents, it is clear that Africa faces severe structural deficits and lags behind other developing countries over the past two decades, with implications for FDI inflows (table 4). Cantwell (1997), for example, has suggested that most African countries lack the skill and technological infrastructure to effectively absorb larger flows of FDI even in the primary sector; and Lall (2004) sees the lack of "technological effort" in Africa as cutting it off from the most dynamic components of global FDI flows in manufacturing.

Table 4

AFRICA'S TECHNOLOGY GAP

Group or region	Skills		Technological effort		Technology imports		ICT Infrastructure	
	Tertiary technical enrolment (per 1,000 of pop.)		R&D per capita ($)		Royalties and technical fees per capita ($)		Telephone mainlines (per 1,000 of pop.)	Personal computers (per 1,000 of pop.)
	1985	1998	1985	1998	1985	1998	1998	1998
World	**11.1**	**14.6**	**22.9**	**71.4**	**2.6**	**14.2**	**152.5**	**64.9**
Industrialized countries	34.3	40.1	122.3	402.4	12.0	66.2	571.1	316.5
Transition economies	..	26.3	..	8.8	..	2.5	214.0	42.7
Developing countries	6.3	8.7	0.6	4.6	0.6	3.9	62.6	14.2
East Asia	4.6	9.2	...	8.7	..	7.1	82.7	19.3
East Asia less China	12.3	21.9	3.2	31.0	2.7	26.6	119.3	48.6
South Asia	5.1	5.4	0.3	0.3	-	0.2	19.7	2.6
Latin America and the Caribbean	16.6	17.3	1.1	6.3	1.9	5.3	122.3	33.3
Sub-Saharan Africa	..	4.0	0.6	1.3	0.4	0.6	16.5	7.8
Sub-Saharan Africa less South Africa	1.7	2.7	-	-	-	0.2	5.7	3.4
Middle East and North Africa	13.6	20.5	0.4	1.4	0.1	3	115	14.8

Source: UNIDO, Industrial Development Report 2004: 177

Technological effort, however, is not independent of the expansion of productive capacity, both because technological change is often embodied in new equipment and because learning on the job depends on the availability of employment opportunities (UNCTAD, 2003a: 61–62). In all developing regions, strong complementarities and mutually reinforcing linkages among capital accumulation, technological progress, financial depth and structural change constitute the basis for rapid and sustained productivity growth and successful integration into the global economy.

In the interplay of linkages that make up a virtuous growth regime, capital accumulation holds a central place in Africa, as elsewhere. This is potentially "good news" for Africa, given that, in the right environment, "domestic and foreign savings can be directed toward productive opportunities rapidly" (Freeman and Lindauer, 1999: 9). Previous UNCTAD research has also found a positive but weak relation between the share of FDI in GDP and the share of gross fixed capital formation, but also that a high share of domestic capital formation is generally a prerequisite for the positive impact of FDI to outweigh any negative effects (UNCTAD, 2003a: 76–78). Given a weak domestic accumulation dynamic, however, it is also possible that the two sets of investment decisions can be driven by different impulses. Among a selected group of 34 developing countries examined by UNCTAD, very few in Africa (Mauritius, Senegal and Zimbabwe) appeared to exhibit strong complementary linkages between domestic investment and FDI. Not surprisingly, while there does appear to be a positive relation between FDI and growth in Africa, it is a very weak association and is unstable in the presence of one or two outliers (figure 3). These interdependencies in Africa's investment process will be examined in greater detail in the next section.

Figure 3

RELATIONSHIP BETWEEN GDP GROWTH AND FDI INFLOWS, 1970–2003
(per cent)

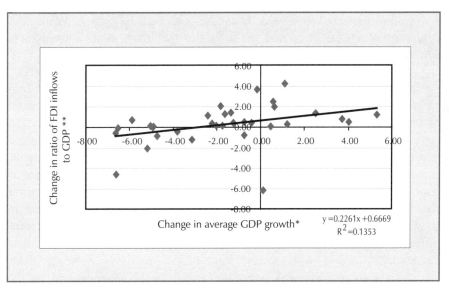

Source: UNCTAD secretariat computations based on UNCTAD FDI/TNC database and World
         Bank online data.
   *   The difference in average GDP growth during 1970-1979 compared to 1990–2003.
  **   The difference between average ratio of FDI inflows to GDP for the periods 1970–1979 and
         1990–2003.

C. Adjustment failures, FDI and the African growth story revisited

Once growth, per-capita income and economic structure are controlled for, Africa does not appear to be an outlier in the FDI story. A simple econometric exercise undertaken by the UNCTAD secretariat shows that a small number of these structural variables are the main determinants of flows to developing countries, and that Africa is no exception (box 4). Moreover, on closer examination, much of the recent improvement in economic performance in Africa is accounted for by a small number of oil-producing countries which have grown at more than double the average for the region, and by a small group of middle-income economies which enjoyed stronger growth prior to the debt crisis and avoided adjustment programmes or had these applied with the lightest of touches (Tahari et al., 2004). Just eight countries from among these two groupings account for almost half of the total increase in FDI flows to Africa during the period 1999–2003 over the previous six years. While this improvement is to be welcomed, the suggestion that it anticipates a new type of growth dynamic for the region seems implausible.

Rather, and as has been discussed in greater detail in previous UNCTAD reports on Africa, the period since 1980 has been one of both slower and more volatile growth, not only in comparison to dynamic developing regions but also compared to the region's own previous 20-year economic record. Strong growth spells have become less frequent at the country level and negative growth more frequent, and the continent has exhibited income divergence as poorer countries have fallen further behind middle-income and richer countries. While specific country factors need to be included in a more comprehensive assessment of these trends, persistently tight external constraints owing to weak commodity prices, stagnant or falling ODA and high levels of indebtedness, along with stalled industrialization (and in many cases deindustrialization) and weak domestic capital formation, appear to be the factors in common.[17]

The last two factors are of particular significance for understanding the scale and impact of FDI in the region. The "growth meltdown" hit African economies in the late 1970s, sooner than other developing regions (Ben-David and Papell,

Box 4

DETERMINANTS OF FDI TO AFRICA: HOW DIFFERENT?

There is a large though inconclusive econometric literature on the determinants of FDI, including in Africa. Much of the recent literature has looked for governance failures behind the perceived shortfall in FDI flows to Africa, and has constructed and tested models accordingly with, inter alia, trade policies, fiscal stance, inflation, financial liberalization and state ownership variously included. The UNCTAD secretariat ran its own series of regressions using panel data for 71 developing countries for the period 1982–2002, including 36 countries from SSA, for which separate regressions were also run. FDI as a percentage of GDP was regressed on a series of structural variables which included industrial value added as a percentage of GDP, manufacturing exports as a share of total exports and manufacturing value added as a share of total GDP; infrastructure as measured by the number of telephone lines; GDP growth and GDP per capita; and a (one-year) lagged FDI variable. Inflation was also included. The estimated technique used was the Generalized Least Squares with cross-section weights.

In general, UNCTAD secretariat estimations produced the expected results in terms of the sign and size of coefficients. The table below shows the outcome of two pool regressions for all developing and African countries in the sample. For all countries, lagged FDI is consistently and strongly significant, as are industry as a per cent of GDP, infrastructure, growth and per capita income, although the latter is sensitive to the inclusion of the infrastructure variable. It is also clear that there are significant country effects, as measured by the F-test on fixed effects. A dummy variable for Africa in these equations was not significant. Similar results were reported for the separate regressions run for African countries. Surprisingly, ores and metals as a percentage of GDP were significant but with the wrong sign for the period 1982–2002. There are also country-level effects in Africa.

Results	All countries		African countries	
	(1)	(2)	(3)	(4)
Constant				
Industry as a % of GDP	0.004*	0.004**	0.017**	0.019**
Infrastructure	0.006*	0.006*	0.007**	0.007**
GDP growth		0.014*		0.009*
Inflation (average last 2 years)	-0.0003*	-0.0003*	-0.009*	-0.009*
FDI (-1)	0.488*	0.487*	0.420*	0.417*
F test on fixed effects	18.2*	243.1*	7.1*	6.9*
R 2	0.62	0.63	0.54	0.54
F	689.0*	529.4*	246.3*	1986.2*
DW	2.11	2.13	2.17	2.17
Included observations	21	21	21	21
Number of cross-sections	71	71	36	36
Total panel	1323	1323	675	675
Sample	1982-2002	1982-2002	1982-2002	1982-2002

Source: World Development Indicators, The World Bank FDI database from UNCTAD.

Notes: * Significant at the 1% level.
    ** Significant at the 5% level.

1995). This can in part be attributed to a failure to diversify sufficiently in the period of faster growth in the 1960s and 1970s.[18] The initial growth spurt in industrial activity in many African countries following independence was already stalling in the mid-1970s; it dropped from an annual average of over 8 per cent in SSA between 1965 and 1973 to just 4 per cent between 1973 and 1980. As a result, by the late 1970s only a handful of African countries had reached the threshold level of manufacturing activity that would allow domestic firms to break out of the vicious circle of small markets and low productivity and build stronger links between investment and exporting, allowing entry into foreign markets. In this context, the shift in composition of FDI flows towards manufacturing was also slower than elsewhere and was usually the result of heavy protection providing a captured market, with insufficient attention to export promotion.[19]

The sharp deterioration in the external environment of the late 1970s and early 1980s not only shattered the profitability of the fledgling manufacturing sector, damaging investment prospects and increasing the sector's vulnerability to further shocks, but was even more decisive in constraining investment in the primary sector, where much production was organized through state-owned companies in urgent need of restructuring and recapitalization. On the assumption that the global recession would be short-lived and that prices of non-fuel commodities would recover quickly, many countries resorted to external borrowing to finance fiscal and external imbalances. This was the genesis of Africa's debt overhang, which has frustrated public investment in physical and social infrastructure and deterred private investment in an environment marked by severe internal and external imbalances. By undermining critical investments in health and human resource development, the debt overhang has also compromised some of the essential conditions for sustainable economic growth, development and poverty reduction (UNCTAD, 2004b).

A vicious downward spiral followed in many countries, with existing accumulation and production structures being unable to generate the growth in export earnings needed to maintain imports, which in turn further constrained investment, diversification and income growth. In many cases, an initial decline in employment accelerated further with increased competition from imports following the implementation of adjustment programmes (ILO, 2003). The growing size of the informal economy in Africa, estimated to account for 42 per cent of output in 1999–2000, although reaching as high as 60 per cent in some countries (Schneider, 2002) is an indication of the near-collapse of the formal sector and the failure of these programmes to stimulate a sustained recovery across the region. An equally telling, and related, sign of the vicious spiral has been the "deindustrialization" trend across much of the region. The share of manufacturing output in GDP dropped sharply in SSA between 1980 and 1990 before stalling at a level in the 1990s below that reached in 1960 (UNCTAD, 2003a).[20] In 1980, there had been seven countries in SSA with per-capita manufacturing comparable to, and often higher than, Thailand; by 2002, with the exception of Mauritius, all had been overtaken. Various cross-country studies have traced this trend to the sharp slowdown of output growth under adjustment programmes. Moreover, these studies also show that differences in productivity and export performance in the industrial sector explain much of the variance in growth performance within Africa over the post-debt crisis period.[21]

For many countries in the region, dependence on commodity exports has, over this period, remained very high, and in some cases has risen even higher, although paradoxically Africa's share of world commodity exports has actually declined. These countries have consequently been exposed to high price volatility, mainly from supply shocks, even as real prices continued their secular decline. The attendant terms of trade losses exacted heavy costs in terms of incomes, indebtedness, investment and development and made diversification even less likely. As is explained in greater detail elsewhere, this commodity trap has become a poverty trap for many countries (UNCTAD, 2002c and 2003b).

Based on this record, it is clear that most adjustment programmes have done little to alter the region's pattern of structural change and integration into the global economy, and, in the case of manufacturing, have almost certainly been regressive (UNCTAD, 2003a, part II). These programmes were essentially designed on the assumption that import-oriented growth strategies could effectively be switched to market-driven, outward-oriented strategies simply by eliminating inflation, downsizing the public sector and opening up to foreign trade and capital. While reporting some degree of success on these measures, most programmes have failed singularly to re-establish a pro-investment, pro-employment economic climate.[22]

This record can in part be understood as a result of linking monetary and fiscal policy exclusively to price distortions rather than to more traditional macroeconomic concerns such as the level and composition of aggregate demand, the state of the business cycle and exchange rate management. As a result, domestic industry has encountered serious difficulties in financing investment both for restructuring and adding new capacity, with banks finding it more attractive to hold government paper or lend to foreign affiliates. Moreover, inconsistencies between macroeconomic, trade and industrial policies have hindered technological upgrading and contributed to weak productivity performance, leaving local firms, particularly the more export-oriented, vulnerable to wage and exchange rate pressures or unforeseen external shocks.

These policy inconsistencies can in part be traced to an unduly narrow conception of a healthy investment climate in late industrializing economies. Previous UNCTAD research has shown that the profit-investment nexus has been weak in Africa, particularly since the debt crisis (UNCTAD, 1997), in large part because the mix of incentives and disciplinary pressures that could generate profits above market forces and steer those towards productive sectors has been missing. This problem has been compounded by the absence of large domestic enterprises with links to domestic financial institutions, which could augment investment from retained earnings with long-term bank lending.[23] Moreover, the establishment of a dynamic profit-investment nexus has been further impeded by declining public investment which could help crowd in private investment, as was the case in East Asia after the debt crisis (UNCTAD, 2003a: 74–76) and has also been true of more successful African economies such as Botswana and Mauritius (UNCTAD, 1998: 125–126).

A healthy investment climate is not characterized exclusively by a high investment ratio but must also support virtuous circles between investment, exports and growth in sectors with significant productivity and market potential. These are sectors where scale economies, technological dynamism and learning economies hold out the possibility of sustained improvement in wages and living standards and offer a more balanced integration into the global economy. However, recent UNCTAD studies have shown that in many countries undergoing adjustment programmes, a combination of rapid liberalization and wage compression, rather than diversification and upgrading, has been the driving force behind more export-oriented growth. Thus, among 26 selected developing countries between 1980 and 2000, wage compression and devaluation have been the principal means by which African economies have sought to improve their competitiveness; the danger is that these countries will be locked into traditional low-technology and low-income-elasticity exports (UNCTAD, 2003a: 106–121). This finding has been confirmed in a study of a larger group of African economies, which finds a structural reversal in the 1990s, back to resource-based exports, and an emerging export profile at variance with global trends, and particularly with the most dynamic exporting regions. Only South Africa shows clear improvement in the share of medium- and high-technology products in total manufactured exports over the period 1980–2000. However, even in this case, the gains were noticeably stronger in the 1980s than the 1990s, and there are few signs of South Africa's breaking into markets for more sophisticated high-technology exports (Lall, 2004).

This weak investment and diversification dynamic has a direct bearing on the kind of FDI that can be attracted to the region, as well as its impact. Obviously such trends will do little to attract market-seeking FDI, and all the less so with trade barriers declining across the region. But export-oriented seeking FDI is also unlikely to find this a hospitable climate, given that low wages are not by themselves sufficient to establish an attractive location. Robust local markets and the availability of intermediate inputs or low unit labour costs are far less important in some other sectors, such as mining, where the emergent profit-investment nexus responds more to external market demands and pressures. When TNCs invest in these enclaves similar opportunities are invariably denied to local firms, whether public or private. But because such FDI has tended to be greenfield and export-oriented, there is still some expectation that it will crowd in complementary domestic investment (Weber-Fahr et al., 2001: 446).

In practice, the links are often quite tenuous. Ideally, the reinvestment of profits or their absorption by fiscal measures and their utilization for the financing of development should provide channels to bolster investment, incomes and savings. However, the nature of the rents generated in these sectors can often divert the efforts of local entrepreneurs away from wealth creation through new productive capacity, into strategies designed for profit capture and redistribution. Manufacturing, which could potentially absorb labour from the informal economy, is likely to be most vulnerable, all the more so where transnational firms are pushing for trade liberalization and there is weak state support for local industry. Not only does this reinforce the tendency of the enclave to rely solely on imported capital, intermediate and consumer goods, it also encourages the channelling of savings into more speculative high-return activities (Mhone, 2000). Under these conditions, capital outflows, which according to one estimate averaged $7 billion annually between 1970 and 1996 in SSA (triple the figure for FDI), can further weaken the kind of profit-investment nexus needed to establish a sustainable growth path. Indeed, some of the largest recipients of FDI have also been those with the greatest capital flight, underscoring the perverse profit-investment nexus that has built up under adjustment programmes (table 5).

Comparative research does report some evidence of crowding in by FDI in some African countries, and more so than in Latin America, although, as was noted earlier, this is not a region-wide result. [24] Moreover, the relation seems to have weakened in recent years, as an accelerated pace of liberalization combined with increased M&A activity, including through privatization, have become prominent features of Africa's economic landscape. According to one recent study, the tendency of FDI to crowd out local investment rose in all developing regions, including SSA, in the period 1990–1997 compared with 1983–1989. [25] A more detailed assessment would need to look to country experiences. Such studies are scarce for Africa. However, a recent examination of the impact of FDI on financial markets in Côte d'Ivoire between 1974 and 1987 finds that the better collateral and profitability of TNCs eases their access to local banks and concomitantly reduces that for local firms (Harrison and McMillan, 2002). A similar result has been reported in the case of Morocco between 1984 and 1992, where it was found that FDI intensified the risks facing firms in sectors dominated by local producers, restricting their access to local credit markets (Vora, 2001). Previous studies by UNCTAD have also shown that financial liberalization and the entry of foreign-owned banks into Africa have produced fragmented capital markets in which access to sizeable credit is biased in favour of larger foreign firms (UNCTAD, 1996a).

A more indirect impact on the domestic investment climate from FDI, at least where raw materials are the primary draw for foreign investors, comes from potentially adverse macroeconomic effects, particularly through an appreciating exchange rate, which can damage prospects of diversification into more dynamic sectors in manufacturing. However, while there is some evidence to suggest that manufacturing value added and exports in mineral-dependent African economies are lower than predicted given their resource

Table 5

CAPITAL FLIGHT AND FDI IN SELECTED AFRICAN COUNTRIES, 1970–1996

	Cumulative flight* (Millions of 1996 dollars)	FDI inflows (Millions of dollars)
Angola	17 033	3 103
Benin	-3 457	394
Burkina Faso	1 266	90
Burundi	819	34
Cameroon	13 099	1 097
Central African Republic	250	90
Congo, Dem. Rep. of	10 099	566
Congo	459	1 095
Côte d'Ivoire	23 371	1 837
Ethiopia	5 523	187
Gabon	2 989	258
Ghana	407	942
Guinea	343	155
Kenya	815	743
Madagascar	1 649	183
Malawi	705	217
Mali	-1 204	198
Mauritania	1 131	97
Mauritius	-268	293
Mozambique	5 311	274
Niger	-3 153	364
Nigeria	86 762	15 658
Rwanda	2 116	233
Senegal	-7 278	379
Seychelles	567	351
Sierra Leone	1 473	8
Sudan	6 983	165
Tanzania, United Republic of	1 699	473
Uganda	2 155	398
Zambia	10 624	1 101

Source: Ndikumana 2004: 357 and UNCTAD FDI/TNC database.

Note: Correlation ratio is 0.96.

* Capital flight is measured here as the change in debt adjusted for cross-currency exchange rate fluctuations (taking into account the fact that a country's debt is denominated in various currencies), direct foreign investment, the currrent account balance plus changes in stock of international reserves and net trade misinvoicing. Nominal values of capital flight are deflated to real values using the US producer price index (base 1996=100) and the accumulated stock of capital flight is computed by imputing interest earnings to past capital flight using US Treasury Bill rate.

endowments, whether or not this can be attributed directly to the high proportion of FDI in mining has not been systematically explored.[26] In fact, a more pressing macroeconomic challenge resulting from rapid financial liberalization in the context of a large existing stock of capital in enclave sectors is the potential for significant outflows and a strongly negative impact on the balance of payments. This has certainly happened in recent years to some African economies where profit remittances have surged above new FDI inflows, sometimes by several-fold, as in South Africa and Gabon (Woodward, 2001: 164–170); also in cumulative terms, for example, in Botswana, Congo and Nigeria (Appendix table A2). While this does not exhaust the full impact of FDI inflows on the balance of payments, previous UNCTAD research has shown that the balance-of-payments constraint did not loosen for Africa in the 1990s even with greater FDI inflows. This situation is unlikely to be eased by the rising share of M&As in those inflows, particularly when these are in the non-tradeable sector.

The bias in FDI flows towards the mining sector is almost certainly associated with very limited backward and forward linkages in Africa (UNCTAD, 2001a) and, while arguably an inherent feature of the sector, the problem is exaggerated in the absence of good local infrastructure (Belderbos et al., 2001). Similarly, while only a small number of studies have tried to measure the spillovers from FDI in the African context, these tend to confirm the wider conclusion, noted earlier, that these spillovers are limited in nature and only detectable in the presence of a robust domestic private sector.[27]

Some crowding out and weak linkages and spillovers might still be acceptable if a "vent for export surplus" and related efficiency gains from hosting FDI translated into a growing number of high-paying jobs. But while evidence from Africa tends to confirm that TNC affiliates pay higher wages, their bias towards skilled labour runs counter to expectations (Gelb and Black, 2004). Certainly, in sectors such as mining, where investment tends to be capital-intensive, there is little expectation that large numbers of unskilled jobs will be created (World Bank, 1992: 28). Moreover, in manufacturing and service activities the overall employment impact is difficult to estimate given that it hinges on a series of indirect effects through suppliers, subcontractors and service providers which are difficult to trace in practice (UNCTAD, 1999a). However, if, as seems likely, the employment effects of FDI are positively correlated with per-capita income, and given the scarcity of evidence on linkages and spillovers in Africa, it seems doubtful that job creation will be a significant feature of FDI flows to the region. This result has been confirmed in an econometric study of 41 countries from the mid-1980s to the late 1990s where FDI had no significant effect on employment in low-income countries and the positive impact for middle-income countries was less pronounced than for comparable levels of domestic investment (Spiezia, 2004), and by various country level studies where job creation linked to FDI outside a small number of EPZs appears to have been very limited (Gelb and Black, 2004; UNCTAD, various years). Again, given that M&As are less likely to create jobs (and more likely to cause retrenchment) than greenfield investment, recent trends can hardly be taken as encouraging in this respect (UNCTAD, 1999a).

Enclave development can assume a particularly perverse form under conditions of conflict. Indeed, a bid for control over resources has historically linked FDI and civil strife in the region, although this need not always imply a causal relation. A recent UNCTAD study has reported an increasing incidence of poverty over the period 1981 to 1999 for a number of mineral-dependent exporters from SSA, with a notably more rapid rise in the period after 1987, as FDI was attracted back to the sector, in some countries, and exports began to recover (UNCTAD, 2002c: 124).[28]

Two points are worth emphasizing from resituating the role of FDI in the broader context of African development over the past two decades. First, as elsewhere, past FDI flows in Africa are likely to influence subsequent flows, and their likelihood of becoming part of a self-sustaining and dynamic investment process with a strongly positive impact on productivity performance depends upon establishing positive complementary interactions with domestic investment in both the private and public sectors. The failure of capital formation to make a strong recovery since the debt crisis, the limited evidence of crowding in from FDI, the incidence of capital flight, and the fact that the ratio of FDI to gross fixed capital formation in Africa is close to the developing-country average all suggest that such cumulative interactions have not taken hold across most of the region during the past 20 years. Under such circumstances, the tendency of FDI to reinforce enclave-type development appears to be a real danger, with external integration privileged over the internal integration of the local economy.

Secondly, the story of attracting FDI through greater openness and downsizing of the state has not been empirically proven and tends to draw attention away from more fundamental determinants of FDI — namely that market size and growth, resource endowments and infrastructure development are consistently among the most significant determinants of the pattern of FDI flows to Africa. While this is very much in line with the broader body of evidence, which finds that FDI is a lagging rather than a lead factor in the development process, the implications do not appear to have been adequately incorporated into development policy discussions, particularly for Africa.[29]

It also follows that simply pointing to the higher returns on FDI in Africa as indicative of missed investment opportunities is a misleading guide to policy makers.[30] Such numbers — to the extent they are reliable — indicate that from the firm's point of view, FDI is attracted to high-risk sectors with the possibility of sizeable rents; from the country's point of view, it means that FDI is an expensive way of financing development which can be of benefit if it generates significant government revenues but can only be really justified over the longer run if it brings significant technological spillovers and jobs. If not, FDI is likely to reproduce a low-level development trap, where the conditions that attract it are not necessarily the same as those required for faster capital formation, in either the private or public sectors.

D. Some sectoral experiences with FDI in Africa

None of the discussion to date should be taken to imply that FDI should be abandoned in designing development strategies for Africa. But it does suggest that existing approaches to attracting FDI in the expectation that these will kick-start domestic capital formation and strengthen productivity performance have not been successful. As such, future efforts to harness the potential contribution of FDI require a shift in perspective to how it can better serve development goals in light of the structural constraints and resource gaps facing the region. The place to begin that discussion is probably at the sectoral level.

The following discussion will focus on cases from the primary and secondary sectors. This choice is dictated in part by a recognition that in the broader picture of structural change and development these sectors are the driving forces of sustainable growth in most countries, but also by the fact that more detailed evidence on the impact of recent FDI into the tertiary sector in Africa is difficult to come by (UNCTAD, 2004). In the face of recent increased flows to this sector, linked particularly to the privatization of public services, a more detailed discussion would require an extensive primary data collection exercise at the country level, which is beyond the scope of the present study. Nevertheless, privatization and the increasing inflow of FDI into the services sector and its impact deserve a critical analysis, particularly as there is growing controversy surrounding the provision by international firms of certain public services in African countries, such as water, electricity and telecommunications.

1. Enclaves and chains in the primary sector

In assessing the likely impact of FDI in the primary sector in Africa, a distinction needs to be made between processed and unprocessed products. Although there are unresolved classification issues, the former are usually identified as manufactures in industrial and employment statistics but as primary products in trade statistics. Processed and unprocessed primary products can be further broken down into agricultural goods and minerals, metals and fuels, with the latter accounting for most non-renewable resources. A further distinction can also be drawn between static and dynamic products, based on such qualities as export growth and income elasticity.

FDI has historically assumed different roles in relation to these product groups. The immutability of geography, scale economies and high sunk costs, as well as technological demands, have created high barriers to entry in the mining sector and integrated value chains under TNC governance. By contrast, smaller sunk investments and multiple sourcing opportunities have tended to make for a clearer separation between production and processing in agricultural commodities, with control located at the buying end of the chain where intangible assets provide more reliable rents (McKern, 1999).

In the case of Africa, the investment pattern in the primary sector was established under colonial relations, whether directly or through the nominally independent "white colony settlements", but the pattern persisted in the years immediately following independence. However, disappointing returns to the host country in terms of jobs, fiscal revenues and foreign-exchange earnings eventually provoked state interventions, including nationalization of existing plant and equipment, not only in an effort to bolster reinvested profits and help build local linkages, but also to affirm national sovereignty over politically sensitive and strategic parts of the economy, particularly natural resources (Kennedy, 1991: 72). The record of these interventions has been a mixed one in Africa. Many state-owned enterprises have been high-cost, low-productivity operations and a drain on the public purse, often acting as a conduit for siphoning away rents to politically favoured groups and individuals. However, it should also be recognized that a number of countries did make more effective use of their primary rents through a combination of public intervention and market-based incentives, including attracting FDI, ranging from heavy reliance in some cases (such as diamonds in Botswana), to insignificant in others (such as sugar in Mauritius). In these cases, fiscal and other measures were used to channel resources from the primary sector to infrastructure development and to support efforts to diversify into new lines of activity, albeit with varying degrees of success. [31]

Recently, surges of FDI into primary-sector activities in some African countries have been welcomed as a potential source of increased employment, government revenues and foreign exchange earnings, and as a potential catalyst for a more diversified industrialization path. These surges have been triggered by privatization programmes, undertaken in the context of structural adjustment; by favourable price movements for some key strategic commodities, such as oil; and by technological developments. There has also been a good deal of optimism expressed that corporate behaviour and market conditions are, if not actually favourable, at least more benign than in the past.

(a) FDI in the Mining Sector: New opportunities or a "race to the bottom"?[32]

As was noted previously, a large proportion of FDI to Africa has gone into the mining sector. Moreover, it seems likely that mineral (and oil) exports have been a major driver of the recent growth recovery in the region, albeit unevenly distributed. The $15 billion invested in mining in Africa in 2004 represented 15 per cent of the global total, up considerably (from 5 per cent) from the mid-1980s, and putting the region third in the investment league, behind Latin America and Oceania. Of the total investment, South Africa accounted for 48 per cent, followed by Ghana (7 per cent), Mauritania (6 per cent), Democratic Republic of Congo and Côte d'Ivoire (4 per cent each) and some 30 per cent for other countries (*Mining Journal*, 2005). With the exception of South Africa, most investment was FDI. The hope is that despite this uneven distribution, a new profit-investment-export nexus will reinvigorate faster and more sustained growth across the region.

The increase in mining investment in Africa can be attributed in part to major changes in mining codes that have helped orchestrate a state withdrawal from the sector, expanded opportunities for the private sector and increased incentives to attract FDI. These changes have coincided with improving economic prospects in the sector. For much of the 1980s and 1990s, the investment climate in mining was a difficult one and markets in the North were depressed, which resulted in low but still volatile prices for many minerals and metals.[33] Economic uncertainty was compounded by lingering political uncertainty in many developing-country locations, following the backlash against foreign-owned operations in some countries during the 1970s, and in the aftermath of the debt crisis, when state-owned enterprises were starved of resources. As a result, FDI in the sector was driven by a flight to safety, with investments concentrated in developed mineral-rich countries; the stock of FDI in the primary sector (principally mining, oil and quarrying) in developed countries, which stood at just 20 per cent of the global total in 1980, had risen to almost 60 per cent by 1990 and 80 per cent by 1997 (UNCTAD, 1993: 62 and 1999a).

It is against this backdrop that policy makers in Africa were encouraged to liberalize and privatize the sector and provide increasing incentives in order to attract potential investors, thereby competing among themselves as well as against countries in other regions such as Latin America, which had embarked on a similar strategy somewhat earlier and where generous incentives were already in place (ECLAC, 2001). Recent developments, and particularly the growing demand for inputs from some rapidly industrializing developing countries such as China and India, are raising hopes that past market trends may not be an appropriate guide to future developments in this sector. Thus, it is hardly surprising that despite the current high asset prices of mining companies, a new wave of consolidation in the form of mergers and acquisitions is in full swing as investors are more than eager to secure mineral deposits after years of underinvestment.[34]

(i) Deregulating the mining sector in Africa

Among the principal reasons advanced in support of reforms was the underperformance of the mining sector in Africa, characterized by a declining share in the value of world mining output and trade. Poor policies, political interference, lack of investment in geological mapping, poor technical data on mineral endowment, weak infrastructure and the lack of cheap and reliable energy supplies were seen as the explanatory factors. As a consequence, the sector was not making its expected contribution to faster economic growth and diversification. Indeed, its failure to generate sufficient revenues was seen as hindering the wider development process in many countries (Boocock, 2002; see also World Bank, 1992, *passim*). However, a more nuanced analysis of inefficiencies in the state-owned mining sector in most of SSA would suggest that the prolonged economic downturn which started in the late 1970s, along with a collapse in commodity prices following the boom of the mid-1970s, was a major source of rent depletion. In many cases, any revenues generated by the sector were appropriated for balance of payments support, including debt service payments, thus depriving the sector of a reinvestable surplus for exploration, modernization and rehabilitation of mines, needed if the sector was to recover and maintain its competitiveness.[35]

Deregulation of the mining sector in Africa started in the 1980s in the context of structural adjustment programmes, which called for increased liberalization, deregulation and privatization as a means of correcting macroeconomic imbalances, stimulating economic recovery and establishing a more sustainable growth path. This initial orientation gradually assumed a more overt sectoral focus, shifting the World Bank from its traditional support for exploration and production activities, begun in the 1960s, to the commercialization and privatization of state-owned enterprises (SOEs) in the 1980s and capacity building, private-sector development, and attraction of FDI during the 1990s (Liebenthal, Michelitsch and Tarazona, 2003: 2). More recently, attention has been given to strengthening governance and transparency, with the aims of ensuring that benefits reach the poor, mitigating environmental and social risks, and protecting the rights of people adversely affected by investments in the extractive industry (World Bank, 2004b: 2–15). Still, the rationale underlying all these reforms has been to shift government objectives in the mining sector towards generating tax revenues rather than pursuing other economic or political objectives such as control of resources or enhancement of employment, and with privatization as its main pillar.[36]

The reforms are seen as cumulative, and, given the technological and financial requirements of the sector and the absence of local entrepreneurs who might otherwise take over previously state-owned enterprises, for African mining operations to become internationally competitive, the emphasis has more and more been on attracting new high-risk capital from foreign mining companies (World Bank, 1992: 9–12). To do so, the main decision criteria are "a stable legal and fiscal framework, which includes a mining code, contractual stability, a guaranteed fiscal regime, profit repatriation, and access to foreign exchange" (Campbell, 2004a: 17; see also van der Veen, 2000). In return, governments are expected to receive a "fair" slice of increased rents generated in the sector (World Bank, 1992: 10).

Reforms in Ghana's mining sector are regarded as typifying the first phase of mining sector reforms, undertaken in the context of adjustment programmes, and predating the more specific sector reforms introduced in the 1990s. By the end of 1995, 35 countries were reported to have published new mining codes, which have reduced tax levels, eased immigration laws for expatriate workers, and granted tax exemptions for imported equipment (Abugre and Akabzaa, 1998, cited in Boocock, 2002). This was followed by Guinea's reforms, in the mid-1990s, and later by those of Madagascar, Mali and United Republic of Tanzania at the end of the 1990s (Campbell, 2004a). All these phases demonstrate a "remarkable continuity" in the mining sector reforms pursued in Africa (Fox, Onorato and Strongman, 1998), with each succeeding phase building on a set of policies enacted under previous mining regimes and with the World Bank playing an instrumental role in conceptualizing and introducing these institutional reforms (see box 5).

Box 5

MINING SECTOR REFORMS: SELECTED EXAMPLES

Ghana: Ghana's mining sector reforms marked very stringent forms of state withdrawal from the sector against the broader backdrop of privatization, fiscal reform and opening up to foreign firms. However, the mining sector has also received more specific attention. The policy changes initiated since 1986 include the establishment of the Minerals Commission as a one-stop investment centre for mining; the enactment of a new *Minerals and Mining Law* (PNDCL 153); and promulgation of a *Profit Tax Law* (PNDCL 122) and *Minerals (Royalties) Regulations* (LI 1349) in 1985 and 1987 respectively. In addition, the *Small Scale Mining Law* (PNDCL 218) was enacted in 1989 to give legal backing to small-scale artisanal mining in the country, and the Minerals Commission was established as a one-stop investment centre for mining (Campbell, 2004a). These laws formed the basis of providing generous tax incentives to foreign investors in the sector — by some estimates more generous than for other sectors (UNCTAD, various). For example, corporate income tax, which stood at 50 to 55 per cent in 1975, had by 1994 been reduced to 35 per cent, and the royalty rate[a] from 6 per cent of total mineral value in 1975 to 3 per cent in 1987. Additionally, the personal remittance quota for expatriate personnel has been freed from any tax imposed on the transfer of foreign exchange out of the country.

Guinea: Policies governing the operation of the mining sector during the second phase of reforms in the mid- to late 1990s were an acknowledgement of the need for certain forms of regulation (e.g. with respect to the environment), but also illustrate how responsibility for overseeing such issues was imputed to private actors (Campbell, 2004a: 7). Guinea drew up a new mining policy aimed at restoring competitiveness to the mining sector tax system and providing a stable tax regime through the duration of the assigned mining rights.[b] Additionally, the Government initiated the "Program for the Promotion of Investment in the Mining Sector", which would make it possible to: complete the geological map of Guinea; build a reliable databank on the sector; harmonize all legislation governing the sector; strengthen the institutional framework; restructure mining enterprises; and provide

Box 5 (contd.)

management training (Government of Guinea, 1999; see also Campbell, 2004b: 36). Furthermore, the Government reduced its role as "owner and operator" in the mining sector but strengthened its role as "regulator and intermediary". The strategy was based on the assumption that openness would encourage vigorous competitive markets, in which prices would drive the behaviour of firms and so provide for an optimal allocation of resources.

Mali and United Republic of Tanzania: The third phase of reforms was based on the notion that "states do have a role in facilitation and regulation" (Campbell, 2004a). United Republic of Tanzania's mineral code, introduced in 1998 as a result of a five-year World Bank-financed sectoral reform project, illustrates the typical elements introduced in this set of reforms. This code allowed 100 per cent foreign ownership; provided guarantees against nationalization and expropriation; and offered unrestricted repatriation of profits and capital. It pegged the royalty rate at a maximum of 3 per cent, the same rate as in Mali and Guinea, and provided waivers in respect of import duties and tax exemptions on imported machinery, equipment and other inputs. It also waived the requirement (in the 1979 Mining Act) for local procurement of goods and services. In Mali, during the first three accounting periods of production or mining, mining companies are exempted from the following fiscal obligations: *income tax* on professional earnings, investment income and property income; registration and stamp duties; value-added tax and service delivery tax; contribution on patents; and tax on insurance policy (Hatcher, 2004).

a   According to the statutes, the royalty rates range between 3 and 12 per cent, depending on the operating margin of the mine. But in practical terms no mining company pays more than 3 per cent (Akabzaa, 2000).

b   This provision was also introduced in the third phase of reforms, specifically in the case of United Republic of Tanzania, which had a "tax stability" agreement with investors under which the Government would not revise taxes or royalty rates upward during the "full project life" of the mining operation.

(ii) Impact of reforms

As a result of the reforms, Africa has become much more "attractive" as a location for mining FDI. Much of the new investment has expanded the capacity of existing producers, including the development of new mines. However, Mali, for example, which did not have a large-scale mining sector before 1990, has hosted considerable flows of FDI in large-scale operations, as has the United Republic of Tanzania. A number of post-conflict economies, notably Angola and Mozambique, have also seen sharp recoveries in mineral production in recent years.

Corporate objectives have remained unchanged: to maximize profits, minimize risk and recover investments as early as possible. Policy continuity and predictability, particularly with respect to the security of property rights and open markets, remain determining factors. But as tax is considered a cost of doing business, firms will, in part, base investment decisions on the extent to which the tax regime is responsive to the above objectives. Certainly the combination of adjustment programmes and sectoral reforms in Africa has worked to accommodate these objectives.

However, attracting FDI in the mining sector is only part of the story. The other is to assess the impact in terms of wider economic and developmental gains to the state. As minerals are considered national assets and are non-renewable resources, their exploitation is closely linked to the exercise of national sovereignty, and the underlying philosophical presumption is that the owner of these assets should derive maximum benefits from any surpluses generated. Moreover, governments typically have a wide set of economic considerations in mind when designing strategies to best exploit these assets, aiming to maximize the value of locally retained earnings, creating forward and backward linkages to the rest of the economy, transferring technology and creating jobs, minimizing environmental damage and social impact, and expecting firms, regardless of their ownership, to compensate for damages incurred.

Reconciling these interests with the profit-making objectives of TNCs is far from straightforward. Still, at one level, both parties have a common interest in the generation of maximum rents through a "vent for surplus". For governments, this could help break potentially binding savings and balance-of-payments constraints on faster growth in the early stages of development. However, as was noted earlier, the danger is that export enclaves can inhibit a structural transformation towards a more diversified and internally integrated economy.[37] Traditionally, this has led policy makers to focus on establishing processing industries as a way to increase value added and to establish an industrialization path which is less vulnerable to external shocks, and on which more jobs are created, the domestic market is stimulated through various multiplier effects, and favourable technological learning and scale economies are realized (Ostensson and Uwizeye-Mapendano, 2000). While developed countries did see some merit in supporting such strategies in the 1970s, including in Africa, commercial, technological and financial barriers to entry have remained formidable obstacles to dislodging the control of large TNCs (Yashir, 1988, ch. 10).

In addition to export earnings, there is no doubt that the mining industry can bring benefits to resource-rich countries in the form of fiscal revenues. But the extent of these benefits will depend on the share of rents received by the countries concerned and the manner in which they are managed (Davis and Tilton, 2002). At the same time, because of the specificities of the industry, including its capital-intensive nature, relying on FDI means governments will have to balance their expectations with those of the industry in order to provide minimum disincentives for investment in new discoveries. In doing so, governments are invariably faced with choices as to the incentive structure and locational advantages offered by other countries. Consequently, and perhaps more than in any other industry, mining is subject to complex bargaining pressures over the terms of investment and the appropriate tax regime which best reconciles the interests of the different actors involved. Trends in the global economy tend to suggest that the bargaining environment has shifted significantly in favour of mining TNCs over the past two decades (Haslam, 2004).

Furthermore, the mining industry carries with it costs, such as environmental degradation as well as social problems in local communities, that need to be taken into account in any cost-benefit analysis of the contribution of the sector to the national economy and developmental objectives. Failure to consider these costs can easily distort the incentive structure towards a short-term outlook. Indeed, the search for quick returns in the sector can impart a more speculative investment mentality, with generally detrimental consequences for long-term growth (Stiglitz, 2002: 72).

Certainly from the corporate perspective the outcomes of the recent reforms in the mining sector in Africa have been positive, as reflected in the significant increases of FDI in the sector. From the host country perspective, in order to assess the outcome of these reforms, governments would need to consider whether the increasing incentives provided to foreign investors have been offset by the desired outcomes outlined above. Already some observers have described the incentive competition as a "winner's curse" for host countries, whereby investment competition among host countries can trigger a "a race to the bottom" not only in the more static sense of forgone fiscal earnings but also in terms of giving up policy options necessary to organize a more dynamic long-term growth path.[38]

Of course, an assessment of the impact of the reforms would need to have some counterfactual reference point: that is, what would be the likely outcome if mineral-rich developing countries limited their incentive structure in order to enhance their income from the sector? Undoubtedly, there is an imponderable political dimension in the organization of such joint action, as well as issues of corporate response linked to the role of sunk cost, and there will be specific factors at play with some minerals where speculative market pressures are at work. However, one outcome could be that mining companies find their margins reduced and many may conclude that further investment in the sector is not economically viable. This could mean that global extraction levels are reduced, with the result that prices increase on the expectation of lower production levels. With rising prices, the sector would again become sufficiently attractive even in the absence of such incentives.

Still, and regardless of the counterfactual, the tax incentives provided to transnational mining corporations are likely to carry an immediate opportunity cost in terms of lost government revenues. Moreover, they could be considered equivalent to a (hidden) subsidy that developing countries are providing to TNCs and perhaps ultimately to final consumers, while the provision of subsidies to domestic firms is considered anathema to the proper functioning of market forces and is labelled distortionary. Such subsidies are, in general, only likely to be warranted where the TNC uses elastically supplied factors intensively; they do not lower the market share of domestic firms, and there are strong positive productivity spillovers (Hanson, 2001). It seems unlikely that these conditions hold for the mining sector. Consequently, much would appear to hinge on significantly augmented government revenues from the sector over the longer run.

(iii) Revenues and costs

In order to place the various reforms into context, a brief discussion of the salient features of revenue generation through the taxation regime is necessary, bearing in mind that a thorough discussion of this topic falls outside the scope of this study.[39] There is an extensive debate on what an optimal tax regime that ensures a balanced outcome in terms of accommodating both the priorities of governments and those of investors should look like.

Tax regimes applied in the sector are generally based on taxing profits, or the value or volume of production or exports (in the form of royalties), and frequently some combination of all these. While any form of taxation can be considered a disincentive to investment, investors' preference clearly lies with the former, as it reduces their risk considerably. When profits are taxed, investors are assured that they are not required to pay taxes when they incur losses, and that their tax burdens are commensurate with low profitability when prices are low. A number of resource-rich countries apply this regime. Contracts are usually accompanied by forward loss clauses — that is, losses being carried forward to other years in order to minimize future tax burdens — although in a few cases they are time bound.

More recently, however, countries such as Chile, Peru and South Africa have revised their tax regimes in order to introduce some form of royalties. Peru, with one of the most liberal foreign investment regimes, has introduced a 1 to 3 per cent royalty on mining operations depending on companies' annual sales on a progressive basis. Chile has also introduced a 5 per cent tax on operating profits.[40] Draft legislation currently under discussion in South Africa proposes a royalty of 4 per cent on the sales of companies in the platinum-mining industry, and 3 per cent and 1 per cent respectively for gold and oil producers.

There is a range of other taxes such as property taxes, value added tax (VAT) on imported equipment, stamp duty, and so on, that were once applied but have since been, by and large, eliminated as added incentives to investors. Tax holidays are also provided by some countries, although they are perhaps the least desirable manner of attracting mining FDI. They encourage firms to extract as much as possible during the grace period and wind up their operations as soon as the period is over, providing windfall gains to investors and leaving governments with no resulting income but often having to bear the longer-term environmental and social costs. Moreover, because of the enclave nature of mining, backward and forward linkages with the economy are weak, and, owing to the activity's capital intensity, employment effects are negligible. Thus the use of this type of incentive to attract investment to underdeveloped areas (which is the justification usually advanced) may not have the desired effects.

A persistent problem for developing countries is that where taxes are solely or largely based on company profits, governments have difficulty in assessing the level of profits declared by TNCs. As the Chilean experience has demonstrated, through the use of creative accounting practices, firms can undervalue levels of profits in order to reduce tax burdens (Haslam, 2004: 4). Even under the watchful eyes of the best regulatory authorities, questionable accounting practices have been used undetected for several years (Cornford, 2004); indeed, "to assume that such conduct would not be transferred to exploit the weaknesses of a host country's institutional matrix is foolhardy" (Gray, 2004: 8).

The inclusion of royalties in the tax regime is generally the preferred form of taxation for governments, as these ensure predictability of revenue throughout the project lifecycle, are relatively easy to collect and assure income in early and low-profit years. However, mining companies may use various techniques to reduce the impact of royalties. For example, in the case of fixed royalties, firms may alter the annual rate of extraction in favour of future production. In the case of _ad valorem_ royalties, where tax burdens will be higher in years of high prices, firms may be expected to adjust their levels of extraction to achieve the combination of price and royalty levels that will maximize their profits (Otto, Batarseh and Cordes, 2000), although a company would be expected to maximize production in years of high prices, subject to operational constraints and the rate of increase of the royalty payment.

Firms will also usually prefer a tax regime to accommodate speedy depreciation and amortization of investment in order to recover capital costs early. The faster the capital cost recovery, the lower the effective rate of taxation. In the case of early cost recovery, government earnings during the first years of operation will be less and will gradually rise in the later years of production. However, this leaves governments with little income to prepare for and deal with the economic and social impact of large mining operations in the early years. Therefore straight-line capital cost recovery through the project life (i.e. a fixed depreciation/amortization schedule) might be the preferred option for governments.

In order to judge the magnitude of revenues for governments, the cases of the United Republic of Tanzania and Ghana are examined. Both economies have established prominent profit-investment-export nexuses in the mining sector (and principally gold mining) in recent years based around attracting FDI (figure 4). In the United Republic of Tanzania, where gold exports rose from less than 1 per cent of export revenues in the late 1990s to over 40 per cent in 2003, six major mining companies earned total export revenues of about $890

Figure 4

AFRICA'S GOLD RUSH: SELECTED INDICATORS FOR
GHANA AND THE UNITED REPUBLIC OF TANZANIA

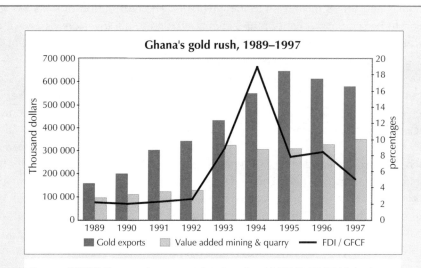

Ghana's gold rush, 1989–1997

■ Gold exports　■ Value added mining & quarry　—— FDI / GFCF

Source: UNCTAD secretariat computations based on UNCTAD FDI/TNC database,
World Bank online data and Aryee (2001).

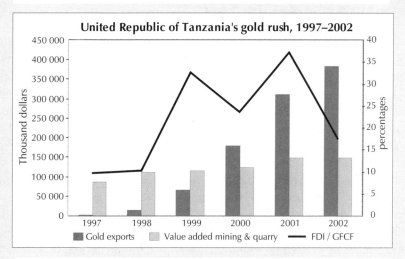

United Republic of Tanzania's gold rush, 1997–2002

■ Gold exports　■ Value added mining & quarry　—— FDI / GFCF

Source: UNCTAD secretariat computations based on UNCTAD FDI/TNC database,
World Bank online data and IMF Country Report 04/287.

million (between 1997 and 2002), from which the government received $86.9 million (that is, about 10 per cent) in revenues (taxes) and royalties. The companies also spent an additional $19.9 million on community development projects and $6.98 million on training workers. The distribution of rents would need to be seen in the light of the benefits accrued to the investors vis-à-vis the income received by the government in order to make a definitive judgment.[41] As an indication, the *Poverty and Human Development Report* published by the Government in 2002 states that, although mineral production has increased dramatically in the past few years, "the share of mining in GDP is still small at 2 per cent. Economic linkages between mining and the rest of the economy, including the government budget, have been limited.... The tax/royalty incentives .... have so far resulted in limited tax revenues, though clearly, increased export earnings have been generated...." (quoted in Lissu, n.d.). In Ghana, where gold exports over a 15-year period (1990–2004) rose threefold, and from about a quarter of total export revenues at the beginning to around 37 per cent at the end,[42] mining accounted for about 11 per cent of total revenues collected by Ghana's Internal Revenue Service. A calculation based on 2003 Government figures of the total value of mineral exports juxtaposed to income (revenue) derived from mineral taxes shows that Ghana earned only about 5 per cent of the total value of exports — about $46.7 million out of a total mineral export value of $893.6 million.[43]

Irrespective of who does it, mining carries environmental and social costs. However, the fact remains that most large-scale mining in Africa is today undertaken by multinational mining companies, and thus they have a special responsibility to ensure that damage caused to the environment and to local populations at various stages of the mining process is mitigated. Such damage could include removal of vegetation (which poses a danger to livestock) and concomitant soil erosion and loss of biodiversity; diversion of water courses and increased sediment load in rivers; acid mine drainage (surface and underground water contamination owing to acidity and dissolved metal content); and land subsidence. Combined with waste dumps, solid waste, and wind-blown dust, these could also result in direct health hazards to populations living close to mines. Other social impacts often cited include, for example, the displacement of indigenous communities and (subsequent) loss of livelihoods, and the adulteration of local cultures. Some of these impacts could be very long-lasting, thereby creating long-term liabilities to host countries. The existence of these problems has been documented in several mineral-rich countries in Africa.[44]

The issue of environmental and social impacts of mining was taken up in the aftermaths of the 2000 Annual Meetings of the World Bank Group (WBG) when its management launched the Extractive Industries Review (EIR) with a view to carrying out an in-depth examination of the potential future role of the Bank Group in extractive industries. A parallel study by the independent evaluation units of the World Bank, International Finance Corporation (IFC) and Multinational Investment Guarantee Agency (MIGA) noted that compliance with environmental and social safeguards remained a challenge, and provided guidelines for the mitigation of adverse environmental and social impacts. This led to the formulation of an integrated strategy to address these problems based on the presumption that extractive industries projects, whether WBG-financed or not, "should not only provide adequate returns to investors but also provide revenues to governments, mitigate negative environmental and social effects, and benefit local communities" (Liebenthal et al., 2003: ix). Taken to its logical conclusion, this implies a proper assessment of the costs and benefits not only of individual operations but more generally of the incentive structures these institutions have been championing (an exercise which has hitherto not been undertaken).

Despite these positive developments, the issue of containing environmental damage from mining operations remains contentious for a variety of reasons. First, many African countries have difficulty enforcing regulations, owing to weak monitoring mechanisms and enforcement systems. Second, litigation for environmental damage arising from extractive activities has proven to be a difficult and drawn-out process (particularly as in certain cases it may involve litigation in home countries of TNCs), so that permanent damage can be inflicted before litigation is settled.[45]

In the light of the growing demand for metals and ores, the challenge for policy makers in Africa's mineral-rich countries would therefore appear to be how to avoid the longstanding problems of enclavism while maximizing benefits from this sector and minimizing costs, including social and environmental ones. This might require a reversal of the current sectoral approach to attracting FDI, in favour of a holistic one that emphasizes the contribution of the sector to much wider development objectives through backward and forward linkages to the rest of the economy, including higher-value-added processing activities.

(b) Agro chains and FDI

The case for diversifying agricultural production in Africa is well established: diversification would help improve the stability of export earnings, reduce the risks surrounding investment and deepen linkages, skills and technological capacity, thereby boosting productivity. As previous UNCTAD research has shown, exports from the primary sector comprise some of the most dynamic products in world trade; 15 of the top 100 fastest-growing exports (at the 3-digit level) between 1980 and 1998 were classified as primary commodities. They also offer opportunities for upgrading to higher-value-added activities that use these products, particularly through processing, which tends to be more technology-, skill- and capital-intensive. However, this is far from being an automatic process, and the most dynamic agricultural products, such as tobacco, chocolate and sugar, which are in processed form, account for a little less than 3 per cent of total developing-country exports, and an even smaller share in Africa.[46]

Building up capacity in more dynamic products need not depend on attracting large amounts of FDI. Indeed, as for example in the case of Chilean timber and fish exports, successful experiences can draw extensively on local resources, including in the public sector (Agosin, 2002). Still, tying into the production chains of large agribusinesses through contract farming, joint ventures or the establishment of foreign subsidiaries is a probable route for many potential exporters (Weatherspoon et al., 2001), and perhaps more so in Africa, where attracting FDI offers advantages in terms of rapid access to markets and technology as well as skills associated with quality control, standard setting and timely delivery.

In the case of Africa, fresh vegetables, flowers, fish, exotic fruits and seafood have been identified as potential new sources of foreign exchange earnings, and a number of countries did move into these products in the late 1980s and 1990s, notably Morocco (seafood and vegetables), Kenya, Zambia and Zimbabwe (vegetables and cutflowers), South Africa (fruits and vegetables), Ghana, Namibia, Senegal and United Republic of Tanzania (fish). While more detailed data on the extent of FDI in these activities are difficult to come by, a survey of African investment promotion agencies undertaken by UNCTAD suggests that these are already host sectors and that more FDI is anticipated (UNCTAD, 1999a: 430–433).

To date, however, FDI has been on a small scale and, particularly in the processed segment of these markets, has gone to a small number of countries. In the export-oriented agrifood business, the investment linkages between local and foreign firms are quite weak, with most producers usually linked up with TNCs through simple contractual agreements or markets. However, for certain agricultural products where TNCs dominate the market, such as canned pineapples and bananas, these companies have either integrated backwards into growing or established closer links with suppliers.

At the same time, higher stages of the chain are becoming increasingly concentrated, with fewer firms, through M&As, controlling the purchase, processing and distribution of major agricultural products of export interest to African countries. For example, in the case of coffee the share of the five largest processors rose from 21.5 to 58.4 per cent between 1995 and 1998, and three multinational trading companies dominate the trading stage. In the case of cocoa, the number of grinders in Europe fell from about 40 in the 1990s to 9 in 2000, and the three largest grinders account for over 50 per cent of the market, with even higher levels of concentration in chocolate manufacturing.[47] Paradoxically, the production side has been moving in the opposite direction. Non-traditional producers have entered the production of these commodities, thereby increasing supply, and as marketing boards for coffee and cocoa in Africa have by and large been dismantled in the context of structural adjustment programmes, chain governance has shifted to major buyers and processors that have moved into operations formerly in the province of these boards. This has created an asymmetry in the chain, with enhanced power at the downstream end and diminished power upstream. Thus producers have moved closer to being classical price takers.

A similar scenario is being repeated in some non-traditional agricultural export sectors. In most Western European countries the five largest grocery retailers now account for over two-thirds of market share, and concentration ratios in food manufacturing can be even higher than this. A similar trend is apparent in the US market. While such retailers have been important in expanding Africa's trade in non-traditional commodities such as fresh fruits and vegetables through increased access to markets, strengthened marketing and distribution channels in the hands of major supermarket chains has meant that the value added is captured by them and reliance on one or two buyers and retailers has increased the vulnerability of producers.

The dominant position in the market has thus provided the opportunity to dictate prices and quality in a market where sellers have become increasingly atomized, and it is perhaps not surprising that producer prices have been at their historical lows for some of these products (although coffee prices, for example, have recently inched upward, thanks to lower stocks in developed markets), even as input prices have been rising (Humphreys, 2003). This combination of forces has often meant that the benefits of liberalization have not been appropriated at the farm gate but rather by firms in the high-income consuming countries.

Case studies of non-traditional exports tend to confirm restricted progress in the absence of more strategic policy approaches to support domestic investment in both the private and public sectors, and while participation in production chains may well be unavoidable for a growing number of products, this should not be seen as a substitute for more effective policy action.[48] Certain complementary assets, in addition to a favourable agricultural climate and relatively inexpensive labour, must be in place or quickly provided if a country is to attract FDI and sustain growth in the sector. Because this will involve public investments in such areas as transport infrastructure, farm advisory and support services, land development, and the transfer of technology and skills, policy makers will need a framework to fully evaluate the costs and the benefits of moving into these areas (World Bank, 2005b: 252–256; Weatherspoon et al., 2001: 10).

2. Manufacturing FDI success in Africa: lessons from Asia

There is broad agreement that sustained development in much of Africa depends on breaking a vicious low-level growth trap linked to commodity dependence. While appropriate strategies will look for ways to diversify into more dynamic goods in the primary sector as well as processing and more resource-intensive manufacturing, building wider manufacturing capacity will be key in the longer run because of the opportunities for faster productivity growth, and because of more favourable market conditions. There is also a recognition that manufacturing offers greater prospects of high "internal" integration in the sense of a denser set of links across sectors, between the rural and urban economies and between consumer, intermediate and capital goods industries, as well as a demand structure that connects domestic wages and consumption to domestic production, and where a political consensus between local entrepreneurs, workers and the government can be forged around a higher-wage, higher-productivity economy (Wade, 2003: xlviii).

Such a pattern of internal integration has been followed by most successful late-industrializing economies, including those from East Asia that attracted manufacturing FDI. Indeed, much of the rationale for African countries to rapidly liberalize their FDI regimes, extend incentives and concessions to potential investors and establish EPZs lies in the hope that such measures will help replicate the success of countries in East and South-East Asia.

Initial conditions in many African economies do not appear to be too far from those present when East and South-East Asia began their respective industrial take-offs (table 6), and the rapid pace of urbanization across much of Africa certainly adds to the case for establishing export-oriented industries in some countries as part of their longer-term development strategy. However, previous UNCTAD reports have warned against drawing impulsive conclusions from this experience with respect to FDI, both because there is an obvious "fallacy of composition" in terms of the potential size of flows that could realistically be attracted to developing countries (UNCTAD, 1997) and because a careful evaluation is needed of the costs, as well as benefits, of FDI even in the most successful host countries.[49]

More importantly, in terms of lessons for African policy makers looking to repair and strengthen their industrial capacity, the picture of regional economic vibrancy across East Asia includes a good deal of diversity in country-level efforts to attract and utilize FDI. Certainly, FDI has been used to access technology and organizational skills, although it was seen as one of a number of possible channels, and not necessarily the most desirable or effective. Accordingly, various policies have been employed to link FDI to a wider national development strategy, particularly in relation to upgrading and exporting; thus, in addition to clear ownership rights, guarantees against

Table 6

MAJOR ECONOMIC AND SOCIAL INDICATORS FOR THE REPUBLIC OF KOREA,
THE SECOND-TIER NIES AND SUB-SAHARAN AFRICA

	Republic of Korea	Second-tier NIEs[a]	Sub-Saharan Africa
	1960	*1975*	*2002*
GDP per capita (at constant 1987 dollars)	768	692	451[b]
Agriculture value added (per cent of GDP)	36.7	28.3	18
Manufacturing value added (per cent of GDP)	13.8	15.1	15
Gross domestic savings (per cent of GDP)	11.6	24.6	17
Gross domestic investment (per cent of GDP)	13	25.2	18.9
Exports of goods and services (per cent of GDP)	3.3	28.4	33
Urban population (per cent of total population)	27.7	24.1	33
Primary school enrolment (per cent of gross enrolment)	103	86.7	87[e]
Secondary school enrolment (per cent of gross enrolment)	42	29.3	27[f]
Telephones in use per 1,000 people	4.4	7.8	15
Life expectancy at birth (years)	53	55	46

Source: World Development Indicators 2004: African Development Indicators, the World Bank, Washington, D.C., 2004.

Notes: a   Indonesia, Malaysia, Thailand.
  b   Gross national income (GNI) per capita.
  c   1962
  d   1970
  f   2000

expropriation, EPZs and fiscal incentives, such measures included reverse engineering of imported goods, technology screening, performance criteria, domestic content agreements, prohibited entry into infant sectors, and exchange controls (Chang and Green, 2003). Particularly in the first-tier NIEs, policies were used strategically in such a way that TNCs had to conform with wider objectives related to profit remittances and the balance of payments, technological upgrading and levels of monopoly control, and which amounted to managed integration into the global economy (see box 6).

Greater reliance on FDI among the second-tier NIEs, closely associated with expanding international production networks in a small number of dynamic exports (notably clothing, automotive industries and electronics), has been seen as a more plausible model for jumpstarting African industrialization, consistent

Box 6

SOME LESSONS FROM MANAGING FDI IN EAST ASIA

An examination of the experiences of the newly industrialized economies in Asia should quickly dispel the myth that attracting FDI at any cost through rapid opening up, liberalization and privatization is the way for Africa to replicate their success. This is true even for the second-tier NIEs (Indonesia, Malaysia, the Philippines and Thailand), which relied more heavily on FDI than the first tier (the Republic of Korea and Taiwan Province of China). Rather, five broad policy lessons with a direct bearing on integrating FDI into successful development strategies can be drawn from these experiences:·

• *Crowding in requires a pro-investment macroeconomic environment.* Profits provide both an incentive for firms to invest and a means to finance investment; in turn, a fast pace of investment stimulates profits. But a strong profit-investment nexus does not emerge from "getting prices right"; a mixture of fiscal policies, subsidized credit and various coordination measures, such as restricted entry, forced mergers and direct public investments, can help stimulate profits and channel them into productive projects. Properly managed resource rents can help strengthen such a nexus in the primary sector, although long-term success depends on building industrial capacity. Large family-owned domestic firms are likely to be pivotal in coordinating investment decisions in such a nexus, often with close ties to local banks.·

• *Liberalization should proceed from a position of strength and do so strategically.* While sustained export growth depends on strong investment growth, export promotion policies, through information services, tariff rebates, tax exemptions, export credits and insurance, also play a role even in more labour-intensive industries. However, longer-term export success requires purposefully nurturing new generations of industry with greater potential for innovation, productivity growth and export dynamism, including through tariff protection. Policies should be monitored, adapted and withdrawn in line with evolving levels of industrial sophistication, resulting, at any given time, in a spectrum of protectionist measures and export incentives. Attracting export-oriented FDI, including through EPZs, is not a substitute for such policies and requires policy makers to pay close attention to the import elasticity of exports and the strength of linkages with local suppliers.

• *Industrial policy matters.* Industrial development involves moving along existing learning curves, including the mastery of available technologies and diversifying into more sophisticated product markets with already established firms. An array of institutional measures and policies is required to improve the absorptive, adaptive and innovative skills of local entrepreneurs and workers and facilitate

Box 6 (contd.)

technological upgrading, including tax and other incentives for enterprise training, national technical support programmes (including for targeted industries), financial subsidies for R&D, science parks and special programmes for smaller enterprises. Foreign technologies can be accessed through various channels, but all require some form of "reverse engineering". Where FDI is seen as necessary, liberalization measures, such as relaxed ownership requirements, combine with technology screening and performance targets, as well as targeted support to indigenous firms dealing with TNCs, to improve spillovers.·

• *Strong and capable states are needed to bargain effectively with large firms.* Managing rents cannot be carried out effectively by "soft states" vulnerable to capture by interest groups (both domestic and foreign). Policy makers must accumulate experience and knowledge and establish credibility in order to bargain effectively with investors. Moreover, because policies can fail, state actors must be able to find out which incentives are effective and for what purpose, discover loopholes and gaps in the policy framework and learn from past mistakes. This requires a stable and competent economic bureaucracy with a degree of insulation from political and business pressures. At the same time, links to the entrepreneurial class assist in the design, implementation and coordination of policy measures, including through sector-specific agencies and consultative councils. State bargaining with TNCs is complicated by their first mover advantages, their asymmetric hold over key assets and a profit calculus shaped by external pressures, which will dictate exclusion from some sectors even as the threat of entry is used to discipline local investors.·

• *Think regionally.* An appropriate sequencing of FDI and trade linkages among sectors and countries in line with differences in population size and endowments can encourage strong regional linkages, helping to marry domestic and international sources of growth. A mixture of market forces, FDI and active policies can help "recycle" comparative advantages, although more formal regional trade and monetary arrangements may better support integration efforts. Such linkages can also strengthen bargaining positions in relation to TNCs.

Source: UNCTAD, 1996a and 1997; Akyuz, ed., 1999.

with the demands of greater openness, new international rules and diminished state capacities (World Bank, 2000a; WTO, 1996). However, not only is a lack of proximity to final markets, including at the regional level, a possible disadvantage for many countries in SSA, but the record of developing countries in such networks is not without its problems and risks. For example, with the full integration of textiles and clothing into the GATT/WTO framework, firms which invested in this sector in Africa in order to take advantage of preferential market access opportunities provided by the African Growth and Opportunity Act (AGOA), are reported to be in the process of relocating their production sites (African Union, 2005). Indeed, the "footloose" nature of the activities that provide initial entry points means that locational advantages are easily won and lost through small cost changes or the emergence of alternative hosts. This is likely to intensify wage and price competition, perhaps more so than when the East Asian NIEs began on their more export-oriented development path (Krugman, 1995; UNCTAD, 2002d). Moreover, because much of the technology is embodied in imported parts and components, with limited local value added and related linkages, there is an added threat from external shocks (UNCTAD, 2002d). This pattern of integration, which shares some of the features of commodity enclaves, can hinder development of domestic supply capability and risks locking countries into their current trading pattern based on unskilled and semi-skilled labour-intensive activities. Consequently, the impact on an economy's balance-of-payments position is likely to be uncertain, varying unpredictability with the share of TNC profits in value added, the degree of import dependence and the proportion of the final good sold in domestic markets (Akyuz, 2004). These risks can be high where trade flows are based on preferential market access and if countries become too complacent about the right policy balance needed to manage diversification into higher-value-added products.

FDI in the secondary sector has, on average, been low and stagnant during the period of adjustment (UNCTAD, 2002a: 52), albeit with some variation arising from differences in levels of development, resource endowments, size and geography. However, two broad patterns of external integration can be usefully identified, from admittedly limited data, which seem to carry a wider resonance across the region. In SSA (Cameroon, Ethiopia and Kenya), manufacturing value added has stagnated alongside weak export expansion and a persistent trade deficit that has grown larger in the 1990s (figure 5). This is a pattern typical of premature "deindustrialization" under adjustment programmes, accompanied by rapid opening up and low and stagnant levels of investment, both private (domestic and foreign) and public.

According to UNIDO's composite measure of industrial performance — which combines manufacturing value added per capita, manufactured exports per capita, the share of manufacturing value added in GDP and the share of medium- and high-technology activities in manufacturing value added, the share of manufactured exports in total exports and the share of medium- and high-technology products in manufactured exports — most countries in SSA lost ground between 1980 and 2000, and particularly so over the later decade.

In some, mainly North African, economies (Morocco and Egypt), manufactured imports and exports have been rising steadily, sometimes exceeding value added by a significant margin (figure 5). Here too, private investment has been weak, albeit punctuated with occasional surges, while public investment has declined sharply. These surges appear to be associated with FDI inflows and have generated competitiveness gains, but mainly between 1980 and 1990, with deterioration in Morocco's position in the 1990s (UNIDO, 2004). This pattern resembles that of other middle-income emerging markets such as Malaysia, Mexico and the Philippines and has been linked to participation in international production networks, particularly in clothing, electronics and automobiles (UNCTAD, 2002d).

South Africa is something of an outlier. Manufacturing value added has consistently exceeded manufactured exports and imports, although it still runs a trade deficit in the sector (figure 5). This is consistent with a more market-seeking FDI in South Africa (Gelb and Black, 2004). South Africa improved its rank on UNIDO's industrial performance index in the 1990s thanks in part to improved investment performance. However, capital accumulation remains weak in comparison to more dynamic middle-income economies. In this respect, South Africa appears to share the characteristics of some other large emerging economies such as Turkey.

Finally, the case of Mauritius deserves closer attention, particularly as it has received the most plaudits for replicating the Asian experience by attracting FDI into its fledgling clothing sector during the 1970s. The island has sustained a rapid pace of economic growth over the past three decades, along with a shift in economic structure from primary export dependence, in the form of sugar exports, to low-skilled manufactured exports of clothing items. Foreign firms have certainly played an important role through their operations in the island's EPZ. However, this has never been a dominant component of capital accumulation; indeed, as a share of total capital formation, FDI has been consistently lower than the African average. Nor was attracting FDI the result of rapid opening up, although a mild adjustment package was introduced in the late 1970s, but one of managed integration with respect to both trade and FDI. During its take-off in the 1970s and 1980s, Mauritius maintained a high degree of overall import protection, including quantitative controls, that was above the

Figure 5

FDI, IMPORTS, EXPORTS AND MANUFACTURING VALUE ADDED IN SELECTED AFRICAN COUNTRIES, 1985–1998

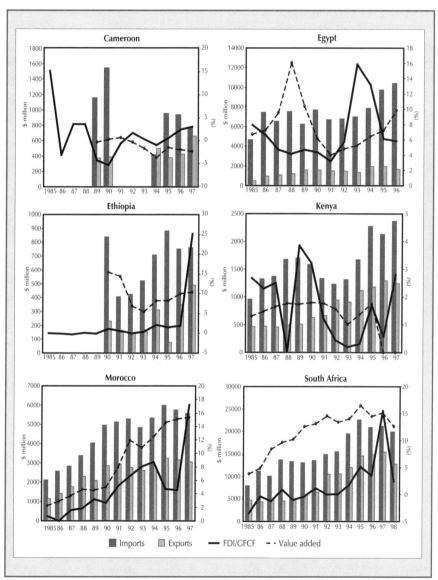

Source: UNCTAD secretariat computations based on UNCTAD FDI/TNC database and UNIDO online data.

African average (Hinkle and Herrou-Aragon, 2001). Indeed, on the various measures of openness considered by Subramanian and Roy (2003), Mauritius only began to open rapidly in the late 1990s, and its trade performance cannot explain its exceptional growth performance. Rather, the Mauritian success lies in translating rents into productive investment and jobs (box 7). This was done through the use of various incentives to encourage investment and exports, through training and social protection, and through higher-paying public-sector jobs. Good management of rents was made possible by a well-paid and competent civil service, protection against arbitrary expropriation, transparency and participatory politics.

Box 7

FDI AND THE MAURITIAN SUCCESS STORY

Over the past 30 years, Mauritius has averaged close to 6 per cent growth, export earnings have risen 250-fold, and the island has maintained a relatively stable macroeconomic climate with inflation in single figures and enjoyed a manageable debt profile, even during the early 1980s. The economy did slow down in the second half of the 1990s but was largely resilient to financial shocks, and on some accounts it is now well positioned to assume a wider regional role (World Bank, 2000a).

According to more conventional accounts, success relative to the rest of the continent reflects a willingness to persist with stabilization and adjustment programmes, along with greater openness towards trade and FDI. This represents a very partial reading. As measured by the share of FDI in total gross fixed capital formation (GFCF), Mauritius has performed well below the African average during its period of strong growth. The establishment of an EPZ in the early 1970s did provide an array of attractive incentives, including low import taxes on raw materials and equipment, overseas marketing support, low corporate taxes and generous tax holidays, and preferential loan schemes, for investors both domestic and foreign. However, foreign firms appear to have followed domestic firms in the clothing sector, albeit playing a crucially strategic role as a source of production and marketing techniques. Reliance on domestic firms and restrictions on foreign ownership have been more prevalent in the island's other key growth sector, tourism (Dabee, 2002: 209).

Rather, Mauritius offers a case of successful strategic integration with a hybrid of features from both the first- and second-tier East Asian NIEs (Rodrik, 1999: 45–48). Key to Mauritius's success has been its successful management of sizeable economic rents. These emerged in the early 1970s when Mauritian sugar exports enjoyed privileged access to European markets, which later expanded under the

Box 7 (contd.)

Lomé Convention, and at a time of rising prices. Although short-lived, this provided an investable surplus for Mauritian entrepreneurs to use in clothing exports. These exports in turn benefited from favourable market access to Northern markets through the Lomé Convention and the Multi-Fibre Arrangement (MFA). Subramanian and Roy (2003: 224) estimate that rents on sugar and clothing were worth 7 per cent of GDP annually in the 1980s and 4.5 per cent of GDP in the 1990s.

Mauritius's success lies in translating these rents into productive investment and jobs. However, the heavy reliance on just two export items (sugar and clothing still account for three-quarters of export earnings) raises the danger of the island's getting stuck at its current level of economic development. Policy makers have been conscious of the threat of hollowing out, particularly as the EPZ has made an increasingly weaker contribution to value added (Dabee, 2002: 203); however, efforts to maintain competitiveness by importing labour to keep wages down and outsource to lower-cost neighbouring locations do not appear to offer a viable response. The problem, according to a recent study by Lall (2004), is that Mauritius does not have the technological profile of other middle ranking economies and is not greatly above that of the rest of SSA. As a result, Mauritius has not only lost manufacturing share in traditional low-skilled activities but failed to gain a greater share of medium- and high-technology markets. In addition, Mauritius has seen a persistent deficit in non-travel services that widened further during the 1990s (Dabee, 2002: 206).

E. Rethinking the FDI policy framework for Africa

According to conventional wisdom, the low level of FDI flows to Africa is symptomatic of the region's failure to integrate into the global economy and a principal reason why its growth performance labours under a narrow export base and low productivity levels. High production costs and distorted investment incentives, which discourage the entry of foreign firms (even where profitable opportunities are available) and bias those that come towards less productive activities, have been attributed to a history of misguided policies and listless reforms. Accordingly, African policy makers are encouraged to redouble efforts to establish a competitive investment climate by integrating more closely into the global economy and becoming more transparent and inclusive in their reform efforts. These reforms promise to attract foreign firms, although heightened competition for FDI also leads to calls for more vigorous, and on some counts better-targeted, promotion measures, as well as the fashioning of laws and policies on intellectual property, tariffs, corporate governance, taxes, labour relations, and technological and sectoral development to match the needs of foreign investors. One recent review of the evolving picture of policy towards FDI recognized that this marks a return to the policy environment of the 1950s (Safarian, 1999). This was a period when much of Africa (and the developing world) was poised to challenge its distorted pattern of insertion into the international economy.[50]

This report has raised doubts about the direction taken by policy prescriptions, on both analytical and empirical grounds. In the first place, there is little evidence to suggest that FDI in Africa (or elsewhere in the developing world) plays a leading or catalytic role in the growth process, and while capital formation must be one of the levers of regional recovery, identifying a healthy investment climate with one attractive to FDI is a misleading guide for policy makers. Moreover, the idea that making life easier for TNCs, including through fiscal and other incentives, is what attracts FDI runs the risk of downplaying more important structural determinants, such as income level and market size, growth prospects, technological capacity, infrastructure provision and degree of diversification. In this vein, the report has argued that Africa attracts about as much FDI as is to be expected given its structural conditions.

Secondly, the kinds of policies that have been adopted in Africa over the past two decades through adjustment programmes, in part with the expectation that these would attract increased flows of FDI, have, by failing to boost growth and reduce poverty, and by stalling diversification and shrinking public investment, actually added to the region's difficulties in attracting FDI. Such programmes have done little to build the kind of profit-investment-export linkages that have underpinned strong productivity performance in successful developing regions, or to move beyond a narrow range of static advantages with respect to trade integration. Indeed, deindustrialization across much of Africa has tended to lock the region into a traditional pattern of insertion into the global economy, including through FDI, leaving an investment-led recovery vulnerable to external shocks of one kind or another.

Thirdly, FDI brings both costs and benefits that must be properly evaluated when deciding on the best policy approach to adopt. Evaluating the net gains will be country and sector specific, with policies towards FDI tailored accordingly and in full knowledge that there will be trade-offs and potentially conflicting interests between TNCs and host governments. Recent developments, particularly in the mining sector, suggest that policy makers in Africa should give more careful consideration to these trade-offs if they wish to maximize the benefits from FDI.

Against a backdrop of increased openness and denuded state capacity, the particular combination of structural, institutional and policy trends endured by many countries in Africa over the past two decades has led towards enclave-type developments across much of the region. In this context, integration externally through FDI has advanced much further and faster than integration internally, and in some cases at its expense. Taking these considerations on board means moving the policy discussion on FDI away from a "hazardous obsession" with openness (Rodrik, 2001) towards a more pragmatic and strategic perspective on how FDI can fit into the development agenda in ways that bring about not only faster and more sustained growth but also structural and technological change. It also means adopting a more flexible approach to how regional and international arrangements can best complement and support such efforts.

1. National policy perspectives

Development ultimately depends on the mobilization of domestic resources for both public- and private-sector investment, along with moves towards a more skill- and technology-intensive production profile consistent with high-value-added activities and strong productivity growth. For most countries, this means building a range of business enterprises, from small independent producers to large professionally managed corporations; establishing a diversified industrial structure; and ensuring a dense network of links across firms and sectors, including through strong domestic markets. However, external resources have an important and at times even key role in filling resource gaps and addressing technological constraints that would otherwise impede this process, particularly in the early stages of development. Access to foreign markets can also help nurture scale and learning economies, both of which are key to a more dynamic investment climate.

While the balance between domestic and international forces will vary across countries and over time, there is little doubt that the majority of African countries have, in the absence of a dynamic accumulation process built around a virtuous circle of rising savings, investment and exports, struggled to find the right balance. As was suggested above, there is little evidence to support the idea that market forces will, left to themselves, generate the desired resources in Africa or provide the requisite degree of coordination. Nor can this task be left to international firms or financial institutions. Accordingly, the state needs a vision of how to combine and sequence the various ingredients of development in light of its own particular circumstances and with sufficient space to fashion appropriate policy instruments and design effective institutional capacities to manage integration into the global economy.[51] Such a vision includes lessons from successful experiences as well as from past policy mistakes resulting from both too much and too little state control and regulation (UNCTAD, 1998).

Behind this vision lies the task of establishing a "developmental state", and while simple blueprints should be avoided, the term is widely used to describe a set of rules, norms and institutions which aim to promote entrepreneurship, profits and capital accumulation without compromising a wider set of developmental objectives beyond those narrowly prescribed by business interests, and that can prevent the capture of policy making by special interest groups. Serious discussions are under way on how this concept translates into particular African circumstances.[52] But in the light of regional trends, two broad and interrelated initiatives probably need to be pursued in most countries. The first is to reinvigorate public-sector investment as a key to kick-starting growth and establishing a more dynamic profit-investment nexus (UNCTAD, 2003a: 74–76; Sachs et al., 2004). The second is to restore a relatively independent and competent civil service with sufficient insulation from political pressures to be free to learn about policy options and to undertake experimentation to find what works best under particular circumstances. Both features characterize the experiences of Botswana and Mauritius, which are among the most successful African development stories of the past three decades. This view is echoed in the Millennium Project report *Investing in Development*, according to which:

> The standard diagnosis of sub-Saharan Africa is that it is suffering from a governance crisis. This is too simplistic. Many parts of Africa are well governed considering the income levels and extent of poverty, yet are caught in a poverty trap. The region's development challenges are much deeper than "governance". Many countries require a big push in public investment to overcome the region's high transport costs, generally small markets, low-productivity agriculture, adverse agroclimatic conditions, high disease burden, and slow diffusion of technology from abroad (United Nations, 2005: 32).

The need for such a "big push" is consistent with the evidence in this report that thresholds in skill, technology and infrastructure must be crossed if countries are to successfully attract FDI and integrate it more effectively into their wider development strategies.[53] Organizing such a push should also give countries more bargaining leverage vis-à-vis TNCs, improving their chances of following their own vision of a preferred growth path consistent with their development priorities.

A developmental state must also be able to mix and sequence policies with the aim of raising investment and diversifying into non-traditional exports. Such policies will aim to raise profits above those provided by market signals as well as improving the coordination of investment decisions across complementary activities, including through support for effective corporate governance in local firms. While the term has been deleted from the conventional policy lexicon, *strategic industrial policies* have a key role to play in this regard.

The strategic component does not, as is sometimes suggested, mean favouring universal protection; rather, it prescribes liberalization, protection, and subsidies in various combinations, depending on a country's resource endowments, macroeconomic circumstances and level of industrialization, as well as disciplining the recipients of the rents generated by such interventions through the enforcement of effective time limits and the use of performance requirements. Similarly, industrial policy, a staple feature of the rise of today's advanced countries throughout the last century, is not synonymous with picking winners or public ownership;[54] rather, it is part of the discovery and coordination process facing firms and governments as they learn about underlying costs and profit opportunities associated with new activities and technologies, evaluate possible externalities associated with particular investment projects, and push towards a more diversified and higher-value-added economy (Amsden, 2001; Rodrik, 2004).

Much of the rethinking on development policies along these lines has been focussed on trade.[55] However, it readily extends to FDI (see boxes 2 and 6 above). This is particularly germane to Africa, where attracting FDI has been the industrial policy of choice for a considerable time, and where incentives to attract foreign firms (through tax holidays, one-stop shop for investment, trade protection, privileged legal status, easing restrictions on entry and profit repatriation, and so forth) have displaced discussion of the appropriate policies needed to nurture local firms and encourage domestic investment.

The key issue for African policy makers is not, from this perspective, whether FDI can bring benefits in terms of technology, capital, and so on, but how the gains and costs from hosting FDI can best be managed to complement the wider set of measures needed to strengthen profit-investment-export linkages and in such a way that internal integration is deepened. This will require policy makers to ask a different set of questions from those raised by efforts aimed simply at attracting FDI: whether FDI raises production costs and lowers profitability for domestic firms; the likely extent of positive spillovers and linkages generated by FDI and whether domestic firms are likely to benefit from these; the likelihood and extent of increased import dependence and profit repatriation; and the potential problems of nurturing future generations of domestic firms in sectors where TNCs gain initial dominance.

Avoidance of such hard questions in favour of easy recipes of rapid liberalization in the hope of attracting FDI will neither achieve economic development goals nor maximize potential gains from hosting it. Indeed, even if the benefits from hosting FDI were instantaneous, which they are not, and the costs minimal, which is unlikely, policy makers would still need to be aware of the longer-term opportunity cost arising from abandoning policy space in a bid to attract FDI and the need for such space subsequently to manage industrialization and diversification efforts. There are no hard and fast rules for striking the right balance, and in any case policy should be adapted to individual country circumstances. Depending on its situation, a country may wish to limit or even exclude FDI if it is likely to threaten infant firms or distort the policy support extended by the government to help them reach scale and technological levels needed to make them competitive. At other times it may be advisable to have an open-door policy with few restrictions, and at yet other times it may even desirable to use an array of incentives to attract FDI into preferred sectors.

Adopting this more strategic approach to FDI will require policy makers to have full knowledge of the policy instruments that have worked in the past and review them to assess their relevance to current conditions. These include restrictions on entry, differential taxation, barriers to hostile takeovers, performance requirements linked to exports and local purchasers (local content requirements), ownership ceilings, employment requirements, and so forth. However, these instruments cannot be used successfully in isolation, and policy makers will require a more holistic approach to how they best link up to and complement other policies in support of development targets and tailored to local conditions.

Some of the most pressing policy challenges from hosting FDI in Africa are in the extractive sector, which still accounts for a sizeable, and in some countries growing, proportion of flows, but where the investment-profit nexus remains outwardly oriented, upgrading has been limited and the challenges of diversification have not been met. The emergence of more home countries searching for raw materials, including emerging developing countries, raises the possibility that African countries will be better placed than in the past to bargain over the returns from investment in this sector. Still, the challenge for policy makers in Africa's mineral-rich countries remains how to maximize benefits from this sector while minimizing costs, including social and environmental ones, and creating necessary linkages with the rest of the economy.

In this respect, the new emphasis by the World Bank on a more transparent management of natural resources (see World Bank, 2004b), should be accompanied by a more fundamental review of (extractive industry) mining sector reforms, including a reappraisal of legislative and fiscal policies enshrined in new mining codes (Acts) in order to increase the quantum of financial resources accruing to the state and communities. Already a number of mineral-rich countries, particularly in Latin America, that have gone through earlier liberalization experiences — and where relaxation of ownership rules combined with accommodating fiscal and regulatory regimes generated resource booms but few positive spillovers and linkages — are re-examining their mining codes in light of wider development objectives (ECLAC, 2004). Indeed, some early starters in Africa, notably South Africa, are revising their mining legislation to bolster revenues, and Botswana, a relatively successful case, is also re-examining its broader policy framework in light of its disappointing degree of economic diversification (Biles, 2005). And in Ghana, a World Bank evaluation of its Mining Sector Rehabilitation Project concluded that the modest amounts of net foreign exchange and high import content, low corporate tax payments, and limited employment creation, following liberalization and deregulation, point to a need for a "broader cost-benefit analysis of large-scale mining that factors in social and environmental costs....before granting future production licenses" (World Bank, 2003: 23). The Central Bank of Ghana has recently reached similar conclusions.

While there is clearly a need for more research to provide the relevant data and clear directions for the industry in Africa, consultations among resource-rich countries about the possibility of harmonizing tax and other policies could go a long way to ensuring more beneficial outcomes for the mineral producing countries and reversing what has been referred to as "a race to the bottom." In the case of Africa, such consultations in collaboration with other interested parties could, for example, be initiated through the African Union, and at a later stage expand its scope to other major resource-rich countries.

Mining companies are generally required to provide an environmental impact analysis, which should be considered by governments before operations can begin. One way of ensuring compliance is the posting of performance bonds (reclamation bonds in this case) in order to ensure sustainable environmental management in the extractive sector. Such bonds have diverse applications, but among the most important ones are to ensure the application of sound environmental techniques during operation and rehabilitation of the sites, particularly at closure. This adheres to the "polluter pays principle" and should be internalized by enterprises in their cost of production (Otto, Batarseh and Cordes, 2000). While the industry is increasingly realizing that it is in its own interest to be mindful of the environmental and social impact of its operations through initiatives introduced, for example, by the International Council on Mining and Metals, this does not obviate the necessity for a strong regulatory regime with efficient oversight capacities and sufficient guarantees to ensure compliance.

Over the medium term, reversing the premature deindustrialization that has scarred the Africa region over the past two decades will be key to shifting resources away from traditional low-productivity activities and attracting a more dynamic type of FDI. This can only be done if a more robust domestic accumulation process is established across the region. This will require enhanced "macropolicy space", including *inter alia* selective capital controls, fiscal incentives, intermediate exchange rate regimes and some monetary policy autonomy, a space in which real economy goals can be given priority over financial economy goals (Bradford, 2005). Initial expansion in many African countries will be in sectors with a high resource and/or unskilled labour content. This will likely involve less demanding technologies which may be most economically sourced through imported capital goods, licensing or means other than FDI. Indeed, given that the broad body of evidence suggests that export success involves self-selection by strongly performing domestic firms, policies towards FDI need to be strategically linked to trade policy, involving selective liberalization and differentiated tariff structures, duty drawback schemes, and fiscal, credit and other incentives to exporters (UNCTAD, 1998).

Attracting FDI into international production networks might still be a desirable option in some circumstances, including in the context of EPZs. Indeed, UNIDO (2004) suggests that these could still offer an appropriate setting for policy makers in some African countries to devise incentives and deliver public goods with a large development impact. However, the poor record with many EPZs in Africa and the danger of enclavism with production networks means that the policy makers should pay particular attention to the balance-of-payments impact of attracting FDI under these conditions, and should from the outset devise policies that reduce their high import content. Certainly the use of differential tariffs, performance requirements and incentives will still be necessary to establish domestic capacities; and in this respect, it is telling that the LDC grouping at the WTO has asked for continued exemption from the disciplines of the agreement on trade-related investment measures (TRIMs) on expiry of the transitional period. Some developing countries, for example India and Brazil, have also made proposals in the context of a review of implementation issues on TRIMs, calling for specific provisions to be incorporated into the TRIMs Agreement that will provide developing countries with the necessary flexibility to implement development policies (WTO, 2002).

Whether and what kinds of incentives might be extended to foreign firms will, of course, require policy makers to undertake careful cost-benefit evaluations. A recent study for the G24 concludes from a number of case studies that the use of subsidies should only hinge on direct evidence of large positive spillovers (Hanson, 2001). Again, the implication for African policy makers, given that spillovers are sector- and country-specific, is that competently trained officials working on investment issues must give at least as much attention to the impact of FDI as to its attraction.

For countries that have a viable industrial base, the policy challenge is likely to be one of dealing with the squeeze on profits and investment opportunities from emerging lower-cost producers on the one hand and higher-technology producers on the other. In this context, upgrading strategies will likely involve attracting FDI into chosen sectors. However, the idea that industrial policy should be designed around this is particularly misleading, and hosting FDI is only likely to pay dividends in relation to a broader set of policies to raise the technological skills of local producers (Lall, 2004). Robert Wade (2003: xxi), drawing on the case of Taiwan Province of China, has suggested that a combination of targeted public investment (including in support of sectoral industrial policy) and "lower-powered" "nudging policies" across sectors involving a mix of consultation, fiscal incentives, strategic tariff protection and close monitoring of import use is the policy combination most likely to ensure a more diversified economy. In this respect the case for performance requirements for TNCs needs to be revisited, particularly where intellectual property issues are involved (Mody, 2004) along with institutional support facilities to bolster domestic value added and build complementary linkages (Rasiah, 1998).

While this report has not examined the links between FDI and the service sector, the need for a more strategic approach seems no less likely. As cautioned by UNCTAD, there is need for judicious domestic policy reform and careful international commitments if the potential for development-enhancing services is to materialize (UNCTAD, 2005b; see also UNCTAD, 2000b). Indeed, the conclusions of the World Bank's recent assessment of its own contributions to poverty reduction in this area are worth repeating:

In developing countries, private investment in infrastructure did not deliver the expected economic gains. It was concentrated in only a few sectors (especially telecommunications), unevenly distributed among developing countries, and dropped sharply after the Asian crisis…The critical challenges are now viewed to be the design and implementation of stable and effective regulation that takes in to account which segments of each infrastructure sector are naturally monopolistic, and the design of pricing policies and subsidy mechanisms to increase access to affordable services for previously unserved customers, generally the poorest (World Bank, 2005c: 30).

Just how much independence, in light of multilateral trade rules, is still available to policy makers in Africa to design appropriate regulations, pricing policies and subsidy mechanisms to achieve their development goals is taken up in the final section below.

2. Regional initiatives

Given the small size of many African economies, there is broad agreement that rapid export growth must be an essential component in the design of their development strategies. However, export shares in Africa are within the usual norms for countries of equivalent size and income levels; indeed, by some estimates Africa trades too much rather than too little (Rodrik, 1999). The problem across much of SSA is less one of trade-orientation per se, and more a developmental problem, common to many small commodity-dependent export economies, of remaining highly vulnerable to external shocks and unfavourable market trends, and where establishing a strong investment-export nexus in non-traditional activities has proved particularly elusive. In part, this reflects geographical handicaps, but inadequate institutional and policy measures in support of diversification have been more important. As was discussed in the previous section, a more strategic approach to trade policy has been recognized as an essential ingredient. But regional trade arrangements (RTAs) have also been raised as a possible response to Africa's poor trade performance and associated development problems.[56]

Such arrangements have assumed increasing strategic importance and proliferated in recent years despite the strengthening of the multilateral trading system via the WTO.[57] In all there are now some 15 RTAs on the continent, and about half of countries belong to two regional groupings and 20 to three, with only six countries belonging to just one group (Karingi et al., 2005: 19).[58] Research by the UNCTAD secretariat has shown that such arrangements are likely to be strongly trade expanding for developing regions generally, and for SSA in particular, increasing both intra-regional trade and trade with third countries (Cernat, 2001 and 2003).

In light of the importance of market size to potential foreign investors, it also seems likely that such arrangements could be helpful in attracting FDI. According to a recent IMF Working Paper on South-South trade arrangements, regional market size has had a strongly positive impact in this respect, and increasingly so during the 1990s (Jaunette, 2004). A simulation exercise for three North African economies using data from 1980 to 1999 found that an RTA would lead to across-the-board increases in FDI stock amounting to 62 per cent in Algeria, 85 per cent in Morocco and 165 per cent in Tunisia. South-South FDI might be favoured in such arrangements given the familiarity of TNCs from developing countries with the host economic environment (Akyut and Ratha, 2003: 158). It has also been suggested that such South-South FDI could be more stable than its Northern counterpart, more diversified and carries larger spillovers, although it is also likely to be concentrated in a few countries and sectors (see box 1). At present, FDI flows from Asia to Africa amount to about 10 per cent of the total FDI inflows to Africa representing some $1.6 billion in 2002 (up from a mere $42 million in 1990). More than 95 per cent of this is from Malaysia and India. In contrast to the traditional sources of FDI inflows to Africa, South-South FDI is more diversified, with Asian FDI, for example, targeting manufacturing, service, textile, and apparel sectors (UNCTAD, 2005c).

The likelihood of considerable variation in the size of FDI flows across the different members of regional arrangements could conceivably lead to divergences in incomes and resulting tensions (UNIDO, 2004: 18). There is, however, more to regional integration than the offer of larger markets. Regional cooperation can bring greater financial stability, better policy coordination, improved infrastructure planning and a more dynamic pattern of industrial development, all of which can contribute to a more favourable investment climate for domestic and foreign firms alike. A progressively deeper regional division of labour, where trade and investment flows link countries at different levels of development, has been an important part of the successful East Asian experience (UNCTAD, 1996b), and African policy makers have begun to look to this experience for lessons for their own region.

Political will on the part of governments to coordinate regional policies in some areas and give up certain options in others is certainly a prerequisite for building regional integration. In recent years, more concerted efforts have been made to revitalize and actualize regional arrangements as spelt out in the Lagos Plan of Action and in the 1991 Abuja Treaty, which established the African Economic Community (AEC) at the continental level. Within the context of NEPAD, proposals have been made to rationalize the myriad of RTAs currently in existence down to just seven considered as the building blocks of the AEC.[59] In addition, there has been a renewed emphasis on building regional infrastructure as crucial to the continent's integrated development (NEPAD Secretariat, 2001: 64; ECA, 2004: 36). The United Nations has recognized the importance of channelling ODA into regional programmes to meet development goals; and increased aid earmarked for such programmes could be augmented through more innovative sources of financing, possibly linked to the regional management of resource rents, as well as the productive diversion of technical assistance budgets into directly providing regional public goods.[60]

While it is unlikely that FDI will play a prominent role in the initial stages of regional integration, particularly in SSA, a regional dialogue and efforts at consensus building should, from the outset, extend to related policy issues. This could cover issues concerning harmonization of codes and policies, contract enforcement, tax and other incentives, monitoring of corporate practice with respect to transfer pricing, tax avoidance, and so on.[61] And while every country must be free to operate its system of incentives as it sees fit, it is likely to be in the interests of African countries themselves to reach a greater measure of agreement on the nature and extent of tax and other incentives. In this regard, agreement on a regional basis might be a particularly useful way to start, since it is here that a wasteful bidding by host-country governments hoping to attract TNCs is likely to take hold. As was suggested in the previous section, this is particularly important in the case of the mining sector, where there are risks of a race to the bottom, and where effective surveillance of global market trends and corporate activity may go beyond local capacities. Moreover, disputes in this sector, which are currently handled at the national or international level — for example, at the International Centre on Settlement of Investment Disputes — might also be better dealt with by regional bodies. Certainly, any expertise and bargaining skills built up at the regional level are likely to transfer more easily to the national levels.

3. International agenda

One of the defining features of the contemporary liberal global economy is the growing incursion into hitherto sovereign economic and political spaces by international firms and market forces. While the justification for this trend usually emphasizes efficiency and welfare gains, there is no doubting that for many developing countries, and particularly those in Africa, the resulting process of interdependence propels their own firms into an open playing field of vastly uneven economic resources and power.

Switching to a goal of promoting capital mobility has already provoked significant changes in the multilateral trade and financial systems that emerged at Bretton Woods, where capital mobility was made subordinate to currency stability, job creation and trade expansion. Reforms are ongoing, but the general thrust has been one of expanding and protecting the rights of foreign owners of capital, standardizing and harmonizing norms and policies relating to foreign investors, and disciplining policies which are seen to infringe on those rights (UNCTAD, 2001b).

Developing countries have been advised to adhere to the objective of an open capital account, and to resort to capital controls, if at all, only under exceptional circumstances. In the context of multilateral trade negotiations, they have accepted that owners of intellectual property should be able to restrict access through internationally enforceable rules on protection. They have also accepted restrictions on their policy latitude towards foreign firms in both pre-establishment negotiations and once investments are in operation, and where these have a trade-related dimension, they have accepted that policy measures should be subject to international disciplines within the context of the WTO. The TRIPS and TRIMs agreements and rules on prohibition of export and import substitution subsidies introduced as part of a single undertaking in the Uruguay Round have been singled out as most constraining in this respect (Rodrik, 2004). On the other hand, the General Agreement on Trade in Services (GATS) is considered development oriented as it has some provisions relating to investment protection (such as payments and transfers, and a balance of payments clause) and adopts a "positive list"[62] (South Centre, 1997: 9–10 and 2000: 11). However, further moves towards liberalisation, with respect to industrial tariffs, and within the framework of GATS, may also constrain the ability of policy makers to choose their own paths (Das, 2005). The expectation is that, by undertaking these obligations, developing countries will receive increased FDI and technology flows, but there is no empirical evidence that this has taken place to date.[63]

Just how constraining these rules can be on African development deserves more research. Certainly many countries have, over the past two decades, failed to reach, or have actually fallen further below, the levels of industrial and technological capacity where these rules might become seriously constraining (UNCTAD, 2002c: 198–199). Nevertheless, trade policy advice to low-income African countries, including in negotiations falling outside the WTO, often continues to push beyond that established at the multilateral level on the assumption that openness will in itself generate conditions conducive to the most efficient allocation of resources, irrespective of whether it is reciprocated or not. Such logic is dubious (Akyuz, 2005), and its extension to FDI, in the context of bilateral and regional investment treaties and agreements, and particularly since investment was removed from the multilateral trade negotiations at Cancún, should be approached with a good deal of caution. African policy makers have expressed some serious reservations on these matters, most recently at the Third Session of the African Union Conference of Ministers of Trade held in Cairo in June 2005.

In this regard, it is important that the current process of negotiating economic partnership agreements (EPAs), including free trade areas (FTAs), with the European Union deliver results that are clearly development oriented if Africa is to reap their potential benefits (Hinkle and Newfarmer, 2005), and that it focus on deepening intra-African trade and regional economic integration processes with enough lead time to allow African countries to build the requisite supply capacity and competitiveness (UNCTAD, 2005d). The EPAs should also permit a realistic and phased programme for dismantling tariffs, and simultaneously grant African exports unrestricted access to EU markets (Karingi et al., 2005), thus incorporating some degree of non-reciprocity.[64] The Africa Commission Report goes much further, noting that one of the principles that should drive the Doha Round from Africa's perspective is to ensure that "special and differential treatment works for Africa, prioritising development without resort to legal disputes, with sufficient flexibility to allow trade reform to be achieved at a locally agreed pace — not forced through reciprocity or IFI conditionality — with appropriate sequencing and within the framework of national and regional development and trade strategies" (Blair Commission, 2005: 269).

Thus, it is logical that there should be coherence between ongoing negotiations within the context of EPAs and the Doha negotiations. This is crucial because other EU trade agreements with developing countries in recent years have often covered a range of disciplines, including the "Singapore issues"[65] (i.e. a "WTO-plus" agenda), which have been put aside at the WTO, at least for now (Karingi et al., 2005). Considering that under the Cotonou Agreement, ACP States have to cooperate on three of the Singapore issues — investment, competition policy, and possibly transparency in government procurement — the issue is whether African countries should allow themselves to be locked into disciplines to which they have not committed themselves in the context of ongoing multilateral negotiations within the WTO (UNCTAD, 2005d).

Although largely ignored or underestimated in the past, it is now widely recognized that short- to medium-term assistance to cope with adjustment to external shocks resulting from trade liberalization is indispensable to gaining the full commitment of poor developing countries to freer trade. Otherwise, it is argued, trade liberalization may be resisted and reversed (WTO, 2004: 20). This recognition extends to FDI, where potential costs can also materialize before any benefits are realized. The multilateral trade agreements of GATT/ WTO were traditionally silent on the issue of adjustment, leaving it entirely for national policies to address, but currently an international consensus is emerging that these agreements should include provisions and specific measures to deal with adjustment costs. This is especially important for African countries, most of which lack adjustment assistance instruments to meet increased competition, for which substantial international support is required.[66] The new challenge for the multilateral trade negotiations would be to properly design such adjustment mechanisms, ensure their funding and find ways to effectively integrate them into the negotiating outcomes.

For many countries in Africa, policy approaches towards FDI have been driven by conditionalities attached to multilateral lending. These have undoubtedly helped introduce a degree of policy coordination at the multilateral level. However, this has been coherence in policy means, which has come at the expense of coherence in policy ends, leading to an excessive pace of reform and an unhelpful narrowing of the policy agenda (Stiglitz, 2002: 53–55). While some welcome changes have been introduced into the PRSP process through the inclusion of social goals, the reluctance to adapt macroeconomic policies to the growth requirements of African countries, and in that context undertake a frank assessment of the impact of past policies, remains a serious obstacle to real progress (UNCTAD, 2002b: 59).

Indeed, with respect to FDI, the emphasis within the PRSP process remains focussed on promoting openness to foreign firms as a measure of good governance. The uniformity of views on FDI in these documents contrasts with the broad body of academic opinion, which insists that the benefits and costs of FDI are country- and sector-specific. It also appears to ignore the World Bank's own conclusion that measures aimed at attracting foreign firms should only be introduced once the full extent of externalities associated with FDI have been fully examined at the country level (World Bank, 2002: 103).

This report has argued that a big push to liberalize FDI rules, adopt national treatment and withdraw strategic support from domestic firms has done little to alter African countries' terms of participation in the international division of labour in a way that brings about significant net gains. Indeed, if it is accepted that FDI responds to success rather than creates it, then such gains are unlikely to materialize in the absence of policy space to devise effective industrial strategies that help nurture and strengthen the capabilities of domestic firms, raise the rate of domestic investment and encourage diversification into non-traditional activities.

From this perspective, action at the international level should be geared to ensuring that sufficient policy space remains available to secure Africa's long-term economic future. An immediate challenge is to map out the full range of options still available to policy makers to allow them to manage the costs and benefits of hosting FDI in a way that is consistent with wider development goals. Some measures are still possible under balance-of-payments and infant industry exemptions, as well as through various special derogations to the Agreements and special and differential treatment provisions afforded to some poorer countries (Das, 2003). In addition, a range of policy options fall outside existing multilateral disciplines. These include financial and fiscal policies, government procurement, support for R&D and training and regional development, to name a few. Moreover, because the strategic use of such policies hinges on institutional reforms which are needed to give policy makers greater influence over the scale and direction of productive investment, building an effective bureaucratic tradition subject to democratic accountability is an integral part of a more effective industrial policy. Accordingly, strengthening state capacities (human resources, institutional and regulatory frameworks) needs to become an integral part of the technical assistance programmes for African countries in order to help devise appropriate trade and industrial policies adapted to their specific conditions and requirements. This should include enhancing their capacities to bargain more effectively with foreign firms through the promotion of comprehensive cost-benefit frameworks, as well as appropriately crafted competition, labour and tax laws which are designed for greater developmental impact.

The international agenda with respect to FDI is not an exclusively multilateral affair. Indeed, a good deal of discussion in recent years has focussed on what home countries can do to interest their own TNCs in investment opportunities in poorer countries, by extending information services and incentives and looking at ways of mitigating risks (UNCTAD, 1999d). Evidence on the impact of such measures is rather limited, particularly in Africa. But on some assessments, these approaches could be made more effective if they were extended to domestic firms, beginning in post-conflict countries where investment risks are particularly high, and including improved funding of multilateral bodies such as MIGA that have previously dealt only with foreign investors (Blair Commission, 2005: 232). Acknowledging this de facto case for industrial policy should help underscore the legitimate need for greater policy space in African countries, including measures outlined above in support of local firms and industries. The Blair Commission Report has also recognized that the quality of government intervention hinges on strong local state capacities and that past policies that undermined those capacities need to be avoided, insisting instead that "Governments and donors must adopt a creative and flexible approach to promoting long-term growth, with the precise mix of policies reflecting the country context (Blair Commission, 2005: 231). The UK Government has begun to act on such concerns by delinking ODA from policy conditionalities.

Developed home country governments might also look at independent monitoring and auditing of their own TNCs, particularly in sensitive sectors, holding them accountable to higher standards of corporate responsibility, sharing information gathered with host country policy makers, and designing disciplinary measures and compensation schemes where there is clear evidence of damage to the host economy. The Corporate Code of Conduct Bill regarding Australian corporations operating abroad introduced in the Australian Senate is, for example, an important step in this direction.[67] The principles embodied in the United Kingdom's Extractive Industries Transparency Initiative, which call for the prudent management of natural resource wealth for sustainable economic development in resource-rich countries, address some of these concerns (DFID, 2005).

F. Conclusions

In order to achieve the Millennium Development Goals by 2015, Africa needs to grow at an annual rate of at least 7 per cent. While several countries have posted such growth rates since the mid-1990s, these results have been episodic, with few being sustained over long periods, and remain closely bound to changes in external conditions. Since the end of 2003, these changes have included a favourable rise in commodity prices, in particular for fuels and minerals. But dependence on commodities for sustained growth has proven to be a mixed blessing in the past, in part because commodity booms tend to have been shorter than subsequent slumps, and because such booms, particularly when improperly managed, have had a distorting effect on other parts of the productive economy. Accordingly, and even if commodity markets can offer African producers a more favourable future, policies are still needed to address structural constraints that have hindered diversification of the economic base.

FDI can play a constructive role in this process by transferring capital, skills and know-how. However, not only is attracting FDI not the same thing as development, but it seems clear from the findings in this report that whether it contributes to development depends on macroeconomic and structural conditions in the host economy. To date, and in the context of two decades of liberal reforms, FDI seems to have reinforced a pattern of adjustment that privileges external integration at the expense of internal integration, typified by the establishment of enclave economies. Behind this trend lies a policy philosophy that wrongly contrasts the efficiency of foreign firms with the distortionary economic impact of the local state. This dichotomy is no longer helpful to thinking about the challenges facing most African countries, including with respect to FDI.

In this regard, it may also be useful to recall that in an earlier study, the UNCTAD secretariat argued that an immediate requirement for Africa was to double aid and maintain it at that level for 10 years in order to raise domestic savings and investment and establish a virtuous process of growth and development, thereby attracting private capital flows and reducing aid dependency in the longer term (UNCTAD, 2000c). This call was subsequently echoed in the Zedillo Report on Financing for Development, and more recently both the Blair Commission Report on Africa and the Sachs report on the MDGs have arrived at a similar conclusion. Combined with a debt write-off, this should provide African countries with the necessary "big push" to break out of the vicious circle of low growth and rising poverty.

Managing such a big push is perhaps the greatest challenge now facing African policy makers. Designing appropriate growth-oriented strategies requires much greater policy space for African countries, including more strategic trade and industrial policies adapted to their specific economic and social conditions and development challenges. The danger to be avoided in designing FDI policies is a tendency to confuse the means of global integration with the ends of economic and social development. A more development-conscious framework must be mindful of all the possible channels whereby FDI can impact, both positively and negatively, on domestic economic performance, including through the balance of payments, local financial markets, and market structure; it must provide the means to manage the pro-cyclical and herd-type tendencies of investors; and it must, above all, be situated in relation to the fundamental processes of capital accumulation, structural change and technological upgrading which are the ultimate drivers of catch-up growth.

Appendix tables

Table A1

SELECTED ECONOMIC INDICATORS FOR RESOURCE-RICH AFRICAN COUNTRIES,* 1980–2000

	Ratio of Gross Domestic Product to Gross National Income				Ratio of exports to Gross National Income				Share of mining and quarrying in total value added (%)			
	1980	1990	1995	2000	1980	1990	1995	2000	1980	1990	1995	2000
Algeria	1.03	1.03	1.06	1.05	0.35	0.24	0.29	0.45	33.77	25.64	27.81	43.31
Angola	..	1.25	1.37	1.23	..	0.49	..	1.14	..	32.79	58.75	66.94
Botswana	1.03	1.03	1.01	1.07	0.55	0.57	0.51	0.64	n/a	46.64	35.40	35.86
Cameroon	1.20	1.04	1.07	1.07	0.34	0.21	0.28	0.33				..
Central African Rep.	1.00	1.02	1.02	1.01	0.25	0.15	0.21	0.13	8.26	4.26	4.34	4.05
Congo, Rep.	1.10	1.20	1.72	1.42	0.66	0.65	1.11	1.14	33.55	28.91	33.85	65.53
Egypt	..	1.03	1.00	0.99	..	0.21	0.22	0.16	18.87	4.27	7.92	7.37
Gabon	1.11	1.12	1.17	1.16	0.72	0.51	0.67	0.43	48.23	33.32	44.12	n/a
Ghana	1.00	1.02	1.02	1.03	0.09	0.17	0.25	0.50	1.07	1.87	4.79	n/a
Guinea	n/a	1.06	1.04	1.03	n/a	0.33	0.21	0.24	..	21.87	19.41	22.66
Kenya	1.03	1.05	1.04	1.01	0.29	0.27	0.34	0.27	0.24	0.27	0.18	0.17
Mauritania	1.06	0.95	1.05	1.09	0.39	0.43	0.52	0.44	..	12.33	12.81	14.79
Mozambique	0.99	1.06	1.08	0.88	0.11	0.09	0.16	0.14	..	0.42	0.26	0.40
Namibia	1.19	0.98	0.83	1.01	0.94	0.51	0.41	0.40	37.20	18.85	9.41	12.19
Niger	1.01	1.02	1.03	1.12	0.25	0.15	0.18	0.18	12.70	5.43	..	..
Nigeria	1.05	1.11	1.09	1.01	0.31	0.48	0.48	0.59	29.13	33.68	40.52	38.74
Rwanda	1.00	1.00	1.00	1.02	0.14	0.06	0.05	0.08	1.70	0.12	0.09	0.06
Senegal	1.03	1.04	1.04	1.03	0.28	0.26	0.36	0.31	0.28	0.53	0.84	1.06
South Africa	1.04	1.04	1.02	1.05	0.37	0.25	0.23	0.29	20.53	9.27	6.96	6.81
Sudan	1.02	1.06	1.15	1.05	0.11	n/a	0.08	0.17	..	..	0.45	1.52
Togo	1.04	1.02	1.04	1.02	0.53	0.34	0.34	0.33	11.33	4.91	5.18	4.86
Zambia	1.08	1.09	1.07	1.05	0.45	0.39	0.39	0.22	17.03	10.20	16.36	4.64
Zimbabwe	1.01	1.03	1.05	1.03	0.24	0.24	0.40	0.30	6.93	4.37	2.10	..

Source: UNCTAD secretariat based on World Bank, World Development Indicators.
*   Mineral- and fuel-exporting countries as listed by the World Bank.

Table A2

TOTAL FDI, GREENFIELD FDI INFLOWS AND PROFIT REMITTANCES, SELECTED COUNTRIES, 1995–2003

Million dollars

		1995	1996	1997	1998	1999	2000	2001	2002	2003	Total 1995–2003
Algeria	FDI inflows	..	270	260	501	507	438	1196	1065	634	4871
	Greenfield FDI inflows	..	270	260	501	465	311	1196	1065	631	4699
	Profit remittances	162	179	174	166	176	257	103	315	364	1895
Angola	FDI inflows	472	181	412	1114	2471	879	2145	1672	1415	10761
	Greenfield FDI inflows	472	181	412	1114	2471	879	2126	1672	1415	10742
	Profit remittances	386	536	559	378	653	929	927	1100	1700	7169
Botswana	FDI inflows	70	71	100	95	37	57	22	403	86	943
	Greenfield FDI inflows	66	60	96	95	37	57	22	325	66	826
	Profit remittances	416	657	669	407	607	658	344	909	954	5621
Cameroon	FDI inflows	7	35	45	50	40	31	67	86	215	577
	Greenfield FDI inflows	3	35	45	50	40	31	-3	86	215	503
	Profit remittances	21	66	69	53	26	55	38	16	77	421
Congo, Rep.	FDI inflows	125	73	79	33	538	166	77	331	201	1623
	Greenfield FDI inflows	64	59	79	33	538	166	77	331	201	1548
	Profit remittances	326	458	99	-77	181	466	369	572	378	2773
Côte d'Ivoire	FDI inflows	211	269	415	380	324	235	273	213	180	2500
	Greenfield FDI inflows	189	254	221	380	324	227	273	213	180	2260
	Profit remittances	204	224	227	292	334	284	270	284	248	2366
Egypt	FDI inflows	598	636	891	1076	1065	1235	510	647	237	6895
	Greenfield FDI inflows	588	465	789	1028	327	707	-150	312	-1963	2103
	Profit remittances	228	34	113	134	100	92	28	89	47	866
Gabon	FDI inflows	-315	-489	-311	147	-157	-43	169	123	53	-822
	Greenfield FDI inflows	-315	-489	-350	147	-157	-65	169	123	53	-883
	Profit remittances	236	386	330	177	227	649	317	474	636	3432
Guinea	FDI inflows	1	24	17	18	63	10	2	30	79	244
	Greenfield FDI inflows	-38	-26	17	18	63	10	2	30	78	154
	Profit remittances	23	36	46	60	32	8	46	1	79	332
Kenya	FDI inflows	33	13	40	42	42	127	5	28	82	411
	Greenfield FDI inflows	33	-13	40	42	42	109	-295	28	82	68
	Profit remittances	91	24	38	8	16	29	48	76	33	361

Table A2 (contd.)

		1995	1996	1997	1998	1999	2000	2001	2002	2003	Total 1995–2003
Mali	FDI inflows	111	45	63	9	2	82	122	244	129	807
	Greenfield FDI inflows	93	44	63	9	2	-50	122	242	129	655
	Profit remittances	6	17	19	36	56	76	141	227	240	817
Morocco	FDI inflows	332	322	1188	417	1376	423	2808	481	2279	9626
	Greenfield FDI inflows	332	282	610	412	1253	423	597	434	655	4998
	Profit remittances	101	116	160	143	186	268	401	482	594	2449
Mozambique	FDI inflows	45	73	64	213	382	139	255	348	337	1855
	Greenfield FDI inflows	31	62	64	200	381	139	245	348	249	1719
	Profit remittances	:	:	:	:	6	0	20	28	42	96
Nigeria	FDI inflows	1079	1593	1539	1051	1005	930	1104	1281	1200	10784
	Greenfield FDI inflows	1079	1593	1539	1039	987	915	1103	1281	1200	10738
	Profit remittances	1330	1598	1477	1427	1621	1832	802	984	1316	12387
Senegal	FDI inflows	32	8	176	71	157	72	38	80	78	712
	Greenfield FDI inflows	32	8	69	71	91	66	38	80	78	532
	Profit remittances	62	14	17	45	74	84	73	93	80	541
Sudan	FDI inflows	0	0	98	371	371	392	574	713	1349	3868
	Greenfield FDI inflows	0	0	98	371	371	392	574	688	..	2494
	Profit remittances	0	0	..	..	..	..	..	633	531	1164
Swaziland	FDI inflows	52	22	-15	153	100	90	50	45	44	540
	Greenfield FDI inflows	52	22	-402	153	100	90	45	45	44	149
	Profit remittances	68	50	24	97	54	81	90	77	81	622
Tanzania, Utd. Rep.	FDI inflows	120	150	158	172	517	463	327	240	248	2396
	Greenfield FDI inflows	118	133	156	149	517	48	207	240	246	1815
	Profit remittances	2	2	3	8	17	13	1	2	2	50
Tunisia	FDI inflows	264	238	339	650	350	752	457	795	541	4387
	Greenfield FDI inflows	264	238	339	248	339	451	412	604	541	3437
	Profit remittances	175	314	335	337	398	468	480	473	537	3516
Zambia	FDI inflows	97	117	207	198	163	122	72	82	100	1158
	Greenfield FDI inflows	79	90	34	48	162	-11	19	82	100	603
	Profit remittances	53	46	63	51	35	33	31	30	20	362
Zimbabwe	FDI inflows	118	81	135	444	59	23	4	26	20	910
	Greenfield FDI inflows	116	74	133	444	35	18	4	22	20	867
	Profit remittances	97	94	118	101	105	73	74	77	100	837

Source: UNCTAD secretariat computations based on World Bank GDF online data

Table A3

THE SIZE OF THE INFORMAL ECONOMY, SELECTED AFRICAN ECONOMIES, 1999/2000

	Informal economy to GNP (%)	GNP per capita
Algeria	34.1	538.8
Botswana	33.4	1102.2
Cameroon	32.8	80.6
Côte d'Ivoire	39.9	239.4
Egypt	35.1	523.0
Ethiopia	40.3	40.3
Ghana	38.4	126.7
Malawi	40.3	68.5
Mali	41.0	98.4
Mozambique	40.3	84.6
Niger	41.9	75.4
Nigeria	57.9	150.5
Senegal	43.2	211.7
South Africa	28.4	857.7
Tanzania, Utd. Rep. of	58.3	157.4
Uganda	43.1	129.3
Zambia	48.9	146.7
Zimbabwe	59.4	273.2

Source: Schneider, 2002.

Notes

1 Michael Camdessus, 2000, predicted such a "renaissance" from fidelity to the first generation of adjustment programmes; see also Fischer et al., 1998. David Hale (2005) anticipates a regional renaissance from attracting FDI into the commodity sector, where recent price movements are helping to improve investment prospects.

2 On the role of geographical factors in limiting African development, see Bloom and Sachs, 1998; World Bank, 2000a: 23–25 and 212–219. For a more sceptical assessment of their significance, see Freeman and Lindauer, 1999.

3 In a listing of historically significant investors in Africa compiled in the early 1990s, all, with the exception of Shell (established in the early 1950s), were established before the Second World War; all, with the exception of the Société Générale of Belgium, were from these three hosts; and almost all, with the exception of some trading and food companies, were in the primary sector (Cantwell, 1997, table 2).

4 This section does not pretend to offer a comprehensive survey of the literature on FDI, development and the internationalization of production; further see Helleiner, 1989; Caves, 1996; Dicken, 2003; Blonigen, 2005.

5 For an early and particularly clear statement of this position see Johnson, 1968: 61–62 and 76–78. Johnson attributed the reluctance of developing-country policy makers to adopt this approach to the strength and irrationality of economic nationalism. John Dunning and Raymond Vernon are rightly seen as the pioneers of this approach; for a review of how their analysis has influenced policy towards FDI, see Safarian, 1999. Markusen, 1995, offers a contemporary restatement of this perspective which builds around the "internalization" story. The rose-tinted approach to corporate activity implicit in much of this analysis is not confined to development issues but is a reflection of a more widespread "innocent fraud" found in much contemporary economics; see Galbraith, 2004.

6 For discussions of the growing influence of finance capital on international production and its consequences, see OTA, 1993, ch. 6; Claessens et al., 1995; Kregel, 1996 and 2004; Hausmann and Fernandez-Aris, 2000; Kamaly, 2003a and 2003b.

7 See Gorg and Greenaway, 2001, for a comprehensive review of this literature. Also see Blomström and Kooko, 2003; Glass et al., 1999; Rodriguez-Clare, 1996.

8 On the nature of this profit-investment nexus in developing countries see UNCTAD, 1994, 1997 and 2003a; Ros, 2001.

9 On the specificities of corporate governance in developing countries, see Amsden, 2001; Singh et al., 2004. On the importance of sectoral features and threshold effects in determining the impact of FDI, see Borensztein et al., 1995, and various references in footnote 28.

10 A seminal statement on the links between convergence and openness is provided by Sachs and Warner, 1995; see also Sala-I-Martin, 2002, and Wolf, 2004, for a popular rendition. For critical assessments see UNCTAD, 1997; Kozul-Wright and Rowthorn, 2002; Ros, 2001; Milanovic, 2002; Dowrick and Golley, 2004. It is interesting to note that the analysis of FDI in this context tends to revert back to a capital arbitrage approach.

11 See Wade, 2003: xlvii, on the distinction between external and internal integration. In common parlance, openness refers to a situation characterized by the absence of restrictions on flows of goods across borders, notably imports, whereas integration refers to the extent to which two or more economies participate in the international division of labour through close links in their production, trade and financial structures. Outward orientation usually depicts a strategy of emphasizing world markets as an outlet for domestic producers, and can be synonymous with export promotion, depending on the degree of active support provided by governments to local exporters. Certainly, a number of countries which might be described as outward-oriented have often had extensive, albeit selective, restrictions on imports; and there are some countries that, albeit very open in terms of the share of trade in output, should not be described as export-oriented given their failure to adopt strategic policies to encourage exports.

12 See Pritchett, 1996; Harrison, 1996; UNCTAD, 1997; and Rodriguez and Rodrik, 1999, for further discussion of these problems. In practice, much of the empirical literature on openness and growth is shaped by the desire to include obvious success cases under the "right" policy orientation.

13 On the general problems surrounding FDI numbers, see Sutcliffe, 1998, and Woodward, 2001: 50–77. Various studies have exposed the sensitivity of results on the impact of FDI to country classification; see Blonigen and Wang, 2004. On the difficulties of attributing causality in heterogeneous samples, see Nair-Reichert and Weinhold, 2001. On the heavy influence of one or two outliers in interpreting results, see de Mello, 1999. On the danger of hiding important breaks in trend in larger econometric samples, see Kamaly, 2003a. And, much as in debates on trade policy, very different experiences with FDI, for example among the first-tier East Asian NIEs and between these and the second-tier South-East Asian NIEs, are often lumped together in support of a common policy approach to attracting FDI.

14 For recent surveys of the impact of these programmes, see Easterly, 2002, and Mkandawire, 2004. Kobrin, 2005, has argued that factors other than lending conditionalities, including market size and skills development, have determined the pace of FDI liberalization in developing countries. While surely correct, his conclusion that "liberalization reflects a belief that lower barriers and increased flows of FDI are in the national interest" (p. 30) is open to serious questions and certainly cannot explain why liberalization has gone so far so fast in Africa. For a more thorough discussion of the interplay of neo-liberal ideology and interest-group politics around adjustment programmes, see Vreeland, 2003.

15 In all these aspects, compliance with adjustment programmes can hardly be taken as an independent measure of good governance when the ratchetting up of conditionalities, including on governance, along with the steady erosion of state capacities has itself had a direct bearing on the likelihood of meeting reform targets (UNCTAD, 2002b; Kapur and Webb, 2000).

16 There are also lingering concerns about the appropriateness of the technology transferred by TNCs, but as Helleiner, 1989: 1471, has noted, this is secondary to the appropriateness of the product mix available in developing countries and the role of TNCs and the state in determining what that is.

17 This argument has been outlined in greater detail in previous Africa reports by UNCTAD; see also UNCTAD, 1998; CJE, 2001; Fafchamps et al., 2001; Arrighi, 2002; Thirlwall, 2004.

18 The terms of trade for African countries turned sharply downward in 1977.

19 The idea that Africa adopted a hostile footing towards FDI upon achieving independence is difficult to square with the fact that the stock of FDI in SSA doubled between 1960 and 1970, and that as a percentage of GDP, inflows in 1970 were still double those of East and South-East Asia.

20 Per-capita manufacturing value added in 2002 was lower in the vast majority of African countries than in 1990. The share of manufacturing employment in total employment has also fallen, although less sharply, but fell again in the 1990s, albeit still at a level above that in 1960. For more specific case studies of the negative impact of adjustment programmes on employment, see Lall, 1995; Buffie, 2001; ILO, 2003.

21 See Piper, 2000, and Thirlwall, 2004.

22 Conventional growth accounting exercises tell much the same story, confirming the need to boost investment levels and to diversify economic activity as the key to sustained growth in the region; see Tahari et al., 2004.

23 The importance of these institutional features to sustained growth and development has been stressed for the East Asian story and beyond by Singh et al., 2004, and Amsden, 2001.

24 See Agosin and Meyer, 2000, which in a sample of 35 developing countries between 1970 and 1996 found that three out of 12 African countries exhibited crowding in and four crowding out; and Kumar and Pradhan, 2002, which in a wider sample of 107 countries between 1980 and 1999 found that eight out of 39 African countries showed significant signs of crowding out, and eight of crowding in.

25 Ghosh, 2004. Murshid and Mody, 2002, also suggest that such a result is probably due to the growing share of M&As in FDI inflows.

26 See Ostensson and Uwizeye-Mapendano, 2000. In recent years more attention has been given to an aid-related Dutch disease rather than FDI.

27 Specific case studies on spillovers include Harrison, 1996; Gelb and Black, 2004; Gilroy et al., 2001; UNCTAD, 2001a.

28 In just two countries of the seven in the UNCTAD sample, Liberia and Sierra Leone, the exploitation of mineral wealth has taken place against the persistent backdrop of civil conflict in the period covered, which has added significantly to their rising incidence of poverty and further eroded the tax base.

29 This is the conclusion to be taken from the numerous studies reporting that a threshold level of income, skills, technology, etc. must be crossed before a positive impact of FDI on growth performance can be detected and from the high concentration of global FDI flows; more generally on the FDI-growth link, see de Mello, 1997; Dutt, 1998; Carcovic and Levine, 2002; Lim, 2001; Mody, 2004; Nunnenkamp and Spatz, 2004.

30 According to Plender, 2003; 50–51, the rates of return on US FDI in Africa and the Middle East were 19.4 and 18.9 per cent respectively, compared to 15.1 per cent in Asia-Pacific and 8.3 per cent in Latin America; he rightly notes that structural factors such as

a country's market size, recent growth rate and average income per capita are better indicators of what attracts FDI, that the countries that receive it are often the least in need in terms of macroeconomic fundamentals, and that international business does not appear "uniformly responsive to good political or corporate governance".

31 It is also worth noting that in the case of Botswana, its initial growth surge after independence occurred in the ranching sector with strong government participation (including the use of a marketing board, nationalized abattoirs and subsidized support services) and minimal FDI. As with sugar in Mauritius, ranching benefited from above-world market prices for its exports thanks to the Lomé Convention; see Acemoglu et al., 2003. For a discussion of more successful cases of managing the primary sector in Asia and the lessons for Africa, see Jomo and Rock, 2003, and Rasiah, 1998.

32 Mining as used in this section refers to non-fuel minerals, gemstones and ores, but not to oil and gas or coal. However, the UNCTAD Trade and Development Report 2005 undertakes a review of the distribution of rents in the oil and gas sector including for some African countries.

33 Price volatility for minerals reflects, in part, the weak response of both demand and supply (at least where capacity utilization is fairly high) to price changes in the short run. This means that both the supply and demand curves are quite steep, so a shift in either curve will cause the market price to change sharply.

34 See *Financial Times*, 2005.

35 See, for example, Kumar, 1990. However, it should also be noted from the outset that this experience was not shared in all African countries following the debt crisis, nor in some other resource-rich developing countries such as Chile and Malaysia where the state has retained a more prominent position even as liberalization and privatization strategies have been pursued. Some SOEs such as Société nationale industrielle et minière (SNIM), iron ore and phosphate companies in Togo and Senegal and the Office des Bauxites de Kindia (OBK) bauxite company in Guinea experienced growth in output since 1975 as a result of investments made in the early 1970s (World Bank, 1992: 7). And in Chile, the state-owned CODELCO continues to remain one of the most competitive enterprises in the mining industry and has generated income for the state even when copper prices were very depressed. The contribution of foreign investors to the fiscal income was minimal in comparison, despite the fact that Chile had one of the most liberal and competitive foreign investment regimes in the sector.

36 Thus, the main message on privatization and revenues in the PRSP handbook (see Weber-Fahr, 2001: 446-450) essentially repeats the position established in the early 1990s that "mineral development requires governments to focus on the regulation and promotion of the industry and that private companies take the lead in operating, managing and owning mineral enterprises" (World Bank, 1992: 9–10).

37 According to the "vent for surplus" theory of international trade, first formulated by Adam Smith, world markets can create opportunities to make use of underutilized existing resources and factors to produce greater output for export. As Todaro, 1983: 351, notes, "it is a moot point whether LDC nationals as opposed to the colonial and expatriate entrepreneurs actually benefited from the process in the short run. In the long run the heavy structural orientation of the LDC economy toward primary product

exports in many cases created 'enclave' situations and thus inhibited needed structural transformation toward a more diversified and self-reliant economy."

38 Akabzaa, 2000 and 2004a; Lissu, 2001; Charlton, 2003; Campbell, 2004a; Hilson and Potter, 2005. The idea of a "race to the bottom" accompanying a globalizing world has attracted a good deal of hostile press and carries a number of not always consistent meanings. Certainly its initial use to suggest that in a more open trading system, the entry of more exporters of low-skill manufacturing from developing countries would harm labour market conditions in the North has been widely criticized; see UNCTAD, 1995. However, a rather looser use of the term exists that is more akin to the idea of "beggar-my-neighbour" trade policies, whereby, given increasingly mobile capital, measures to bolster competitiveness by increasing labour market flexibility, weakening regulations on corporations, reducing social provisions, and so on are pursued in the uncertain expectation that this will bolster investment, including FDI, and bring large and positive spillovers in terms of technology and jobs. See ILO, 2003: 117 and Nayyar, 2002: 5.

39 For a comprehensive and comparative study of various tax regimes, see Otto, Batarseh and Cordes, 2000.

40 In Chile, a major debate on the tax regime was sparked by the sale in 2002 of the mine Disputada de Las Condes for $1,500 million by its owner, Exxon, to Anglo American. Exxon had never paid taxes, as it had not declared any profits during 20 years of operation in Chile. Since the sale occurred outside Chile, Exxon's income would not be subject to capital gains tax. Ministerio de Minería de Chile, 2005: 6–7; see also ECLAC, 2003.

41 While data are not available with respect to industry profits as a percentage of exports, and data between rate of return on investment and share of profits from exports are not compatible, a comparative study undertaken by the Colorado School of Mines (Otto, Batarseh and Cordes, 2002) shows that under the present tax regime in the United Republic of Tanzania, the internal rate of return to investors should be 12.7 per cent for gold. The study was based on hypothetical copper and gold mines under different tax regimes as applied by mineral-rich countries both in the North and South.

42 Data for 2004 are estimates provided by the Ghana Minerals Commission.

43 This figure of 5 per cent has remained essentially unchanged since the start of the mining boom in the early 1990s. Data are from the Ghana Minerals Commission. As in the case of the United Republic of Tanzania, cited in note 41, the Colorado School of Mines study calculates the internal rate of return of investment under the current Ghanaian tax regime to be 13.6 per cent for gold. See Otto, Batarseh and Cordes, 2000, Appendix.

44 See, for example, Weber-Fahr et al., 2001: 443–444; Boocock, 2002; Campbell, 2004a; Hilson and Potter, 2005.

45 For example, a lawsuit against Texaco, now Chevron/Texaco, by indigenous communities in Ecuador involves the environmental damage caused by the company in the Amazon jungle. In 1990, after 20 years of operation, the company left behind toxic wastes which have been assessed to be three times as large as the Exxon Valdez oil spill. While Chevron/Texaco does not deny the damage, it invokes Ecuadorean law of the time, to which the relevant industrial standards adhered, and moreover denies responsibility for decisions taken by its foreign subsidiary, which participated in a consortium with Gulf Oil and the state-owned enterprise, even though Texaco was the consortium operator.

Moreover, it argues that Chevron Texaco cannot be held responsible for the actions of Texaco, a company it took over in 2001, or bear the costs of "supposed acts imputed to a firm of which it is not the successor" (ECLAC 2003, Box 1.5). Nevertheless, reluctance to get involved in drawn-out litigation, with consequent damage to company reputations, may represent an incentive to companies to pay more attention to environmental damage, particularly where this attracts wider public attention.

46 Indeed, of the 15 dynamic products identified by UNCTAD, only three involve no or very limited processing: crustaceans and molluscs, fresh, chilled, frozen, salted, in brine or dried; fish, fresh (live or dead), chilled or frozen; and fuel wood (excluding wood waste) and wood charcoal.

47 A similar pattern of increasing concentration has been reported for other products such as vegetable oil; see UNCTAD, 1999a: 243–244.

48 For such case studies, see Helleiner, 2002; UNCTAD, 2003b; World Bank, 2005b.

49 Further on the question of replication, see UNCTAD, 1996b and 1999b; Akyuz, 1999. If Africa had received the same per-capita FDI inflows between 1980 and 2000 as Malaysia, its total inflow would have more than crowded out all FDI to the rest of the developing world during that period. On the costs resulting from tightened governance by TNCs over international production networks, see Rasiah, 1998; UNCTAD, 2002d. On environmental and other socio-economic costs, see Bello and Rosenfeld, 1990.

50 Stiglitz, 2002: 72, has noted the parallel arguing that the strategy to "Eliminate government intervention (in the form of oppressive regulation), reduce taxes, get inflation as low as possible and invite foreign entrepreneurs in" reflects a "colonial mentality" and ignores the strategic approach of the Asian NIEs.

51 The German economist Johann von Thunen long ago argued that savings reflect a society's capacity to imagine a future and create it.

52 For a general discussion of the developmental state concept see Woo-Cummings, 1999; Evans, 1999. On its translation to Africa, see Van Arkadie, 1995; UNCTAD, 1998: 221–224; Mkandawire, 2001; Szingare, 2004; Taylor, 2002.

53 Thinking along these lines breaks with the current pessimism surrounding African institutional capacities. Indeed, and as is clear from a cursory examination of the detailed conditions and demands attached to adjustment lending in Africa, weak states are ineffective agents of reform regardless of the direction imparted to policy. In this respect, the idea that the more strategically minded North-East Asian states offer a less attractive or relevant model for Africa in comparison to softer South-East Asian states which relied more heavily on FDI, is not supported by a careful reading of these experiences; see Rasiah, 1998.

54 Ironically, conventional policy thinking has made "attracting winners" through opening up to FDI a measure of policy success even as it decries any efforts to give strategic support to domestic firms.

55 See Akyuz, 2004 and 2005.

56 Of the 53 countries in Africa, 39 have populations of less than 15 million, and 21 have less than 5 million. Incomes also remain very low: 32 countries have per-capita incomes of less than $500 a year (ECA, 2004: 17–18).

57 Initially interpreted as a response to disappointing outcomes from the Uruguay Round of trade negotiations, this surge in RTAs has since been supported by a sequence of

events, such as the failure to launch a new round of multilateral trade talks in Seattle in 1999, and the breakdown of talks again in Cancun in 2003, but more fundamentally by the change in trade strategies of key members of the WTO (Yang and Gupta, 2005: 5).

58 A recent IMF Working Paper, however, puts the total number of African RTAs at 30, with each country belonging, on average, to four RTAs (Yang and Gupta, 2005: 4).

59 These are the Arab Maghreb Union (UMA), the Common Market for Eastern and Southern Africa, (COMESA), the Economic Community of West African States (ECOWAS), the Southern African Development Community (SADC), the Community of Sahel-Saharan States (CEN-SAD), the Economic Community of Central African States (ECCAS) and the Inter-Governmental Authority on Development (IGAD) (see ECA, 2004: 27–28).

60 On one recent estimate by the World Bank, 40 per cent of ODA is absorbed by technical assistance. See also Soludo, 2003; United Nations, 2005.

61 All regional economic communities have protocols (acts or conventions) relating to the harmonization of some of these issues, but the problem has been with the signing, ratification and implementation. For details of signing and ratification of the protocols of SADC as of March 2001, and of the implementation of ECOWAS protocols, see ECA, 2004: 48–51.

62 The adoption of a "positive list" approach and progressive liberalization suggests that each country can strategically select the individual service sector or transaction that it is willing to open up at a given time subject to specific conditions and limitations (South Centre, 2000: 11).

63 Article 66.2 of the TRIPS Agreement urges developed country members to provide incentives to their enterprises and institutions for the purpose of promoting and encouraging technology transfer to LDCs. However, this has been difficult to enforce and remains "best endeavour".

64 This will, however, depend on the outcome of ongoing negotiations within the framework of the Doha Round, to clarify the content of Article XXIV of GATT and Article V of GATS, which eventually determine the degree of non-reciprocity and of exemption from coverage that will be permitted for developing countries negotiating preferential trade arrangements (Karingi et al., 2005).

65 Indeed, the EPAs envisaged are expected to cover a regulatory agenda to promote investment and competition (see, for example, Hinkle and Newfarmer, 2005).

66 Recent initiatives to address this issue include a temporary "aid for trade fund" proposed by the UN Millennium Project's Task Force on Trade in its Report on Trade for Development, 2005. Peter Mandelson, EU Trade Commissioner, proposed on 4 February 2005 to establish a special Trade Adjustment Fund to "help the poor to trade more effectively and ease the social costs of adjustment".

67 On 24 June 2004, an Exposure Draft of the Bill was introduced before being formally introduced in the Senate to enable NGOs, the academic community and others to resolve some of the difficulties with the original Bill introduced in 2002.

References

Abugre C and Akabzaa T (1998). Mining boom – a gain for Africa? *Third World Resurgence* 93.

Acemoglu D et al. (2003). An African success story: Botswana. In Rodrik D, ed. *In Search of Prosperity: Analytic Narratives on Economic Growth*. Princeton: Princeton University Press.

African Union (2005). "Report on AGOA". TI/TMIN/EXP 11 (III). Presented at the AU Conference of Ministers of Trade, Third Ordinary Session, 5–9 June 2005, Cairo, Egypt.

Agosin M (2002). Export performance in Chile: Lessons for Africa. In Helleiner, ed (2002).

Agosin M and Meyer J (2000). Foreign investment in development countries: Does it crowd in domestic investment? *UNCTAD Discussion Paper* 146. Geneva: UNCTAD.

Akabzaa T (2000). *Boom and Dislocation: The Environmental and Social Impacts of Mining in the Wassa West District of Ghana*. Third World Network, Accra.

Akabzaa T (2004a). African Mining Codes a Race to the Bottom. Third World Network. *www.twnside.org.sg*

Akabzaa T (2004b). Mining legislation and net returns from mining in Ghana. In Campbell, ed., 2004a.

Akingube O (2003). Flow of foreign direct investment to hitherto neglected developing countries. *WIDER Discussion Paper*, January. Helsinki: UNU/WIDER.

Akyut D and Ratha D (2003). South-South FDI flows: How big are they? *Transnational Corporations* 13 (1).

Akyuz Y (2004). Trade growth and industrialization: Issues, experience and policy challenges. Mimeo. Geneva: Third World Network.

Akyuz Y (2005). The WTO negotiations on industrial tariffs: GATT is at stake for developing countries? Mimeo. Geneva: Third World Network.

Akyuz Y, ed. (1999). *East Asian Development: New Perspectives*. London: Frank Cass.

Amiti M and Wakelin K (2003). Investment liberalization and international trade. *Journal of International Economics* 61.

Amsden A (2001). *The Rise of the Rest: Challenges to the West from Late-Industrializing Economies*. Oxford: Oxford University Press.

Arrighi G (2002). The African crisis. *New Left Review*, May–June.

Asiedu E (2002). On the determinants of foreign direct investment: Is Africa different? *World Development* 30 (1).

Basu A and Srinivasan K (2002). Foreign direct investment in Africa – some case studies. *IMF Working Paper* 61. Washington, DC: International Monetary Fund.

Belderbos R et al. (2001). Backward linkages of foreign manufacturing affiliates: Evidence from Japanese multinationals. *World Development* 29 (1).

Bello W and Rosenfeld S (1990). *Dragons in Distress: Asia's Miracle Economies in Crisis*. London: Penguin.

Ben-David D and Papell D (1995). Slowdowns and meltdowns: Postwar growth evidence from 74 countries. *CEPR Discussion Paper* 1111. London: CEPR.

Bende-Nabende A (2002). Foreign direct investment determinants in sub-Saharan Africa: A co-integration analysis. *Economics Bulletin* 6 (4).

Biles P (2005). Botswana: Africa's success story. _news.bbc.co.uk/1/hi/world/africa/ 4318777.stm_

Blair Commission (2005). _Our Common Interest_. Report of the Commission for Africa, Commission for Africa, London, March.

Blomström M and Kooko A (2003). Human capital and inward FDI. _CEPR Working Paper_ 167. London: CEPR.

Blonigen B (2005). A review of the empirical literature on FDI determinants. _NBER Working Paper_ 11299. Cambridge, MA: National Bureau of Economic Research.

Blonigen B and Wang H (2004). Inappropriate pooling of wealthy-poor countries in empirical studies. _NBER Working Paper_ 10378. Cambridge, MA: National Bureau of Economic Research.

Bloom D and Sachs J (1998). Geography, demography and economic growth in Africa. _Brookings Papers on Economic Activity_ 2, Brookings Institute, Washington DC.

Boocock CN (2002). Environmental impacts of foreign direct investment in the mining sector in sub-Saharan Africa. January. _www.natural-resources.org/minerals/docs/oecd_

Borensztein E, De Gregorio J and Lee W (1995). How Does Foreign Direct Investment Affect Economic Growth? _NBER Working Paper_ 5057. Cambridge, MA: National Bureau of Economic Research.

Bosworth B and Collins S (2003). The empirics of growth: An update. Brookings Institute, Washington DC, September.

Bradford C (2005). Prioritizing economic growth: Enhancing macroeconomic policy choice. _G24 Discussion Paper Series_ 37. Geneva: UNCTAD.

Buffie E (2001). _Trade Policy in Developing Countries_. Cambridge: Cambridge University Press.

Cambridge Journal of Economics (CJE) (2001). Special Issue on African Development in a Comparative Perspective. _CJE_ 25 (3).

Camdessus M (2000). Africa can harness globalisation. _Business Day_ (South Africa), January 13.

Campbell B (2004b). Guinea: Deregulation and its consequences for environmental protection. In Campbell, ed. (2004a).

Campbell B, ed. (2004a). _Regulating Mining in Africa: For Whose Benefit?_ Uppsala: Nordiska Afrikainstitutet.

Cantwell J (1997). Globalization and development in Africa. In Dunning J and Hamdani K, eds. _The New Globalism and Developing Countries_. Tokyo: UNU Press.

Carcovic M and Levine R (2002). Does foreign direct investment accelerate economic growth? Mimeo. Minneapolis, University of Minnesota.

Caves R (1996). _Multinational Enterprises and Economic Analysis_. Cambridge: Cambridge University Press.

Cernat L (2001). Assessing regional trade arrangements: Are South-South RTAs more trade diverting? _Policy Issues in International Trade and Commodities Study Series_ 16. Geneva: UNCTAD.

Cernat L (2003). Assessing South-South regional integration: Same issues, many metrics. _Policy Issues in International Trade and Commodities Study Series_ 21. Geneva: UNCTAD.

Chang H-J and Green D (2003). *The Northern WTO Agenda on Investment: Do As We Say, Not As We Did*. Geneva: South Centre.

Charlton A (2003). Incentive bidding for mobile investment: Economic consequences and potential responses. *OECD Development Centre Working Paper* 203. Paris: OECD.

Claessens S et al. (1995). Portfolio capital flows: Hot or cold? *World Bank Economic Review* 9 (1).

Collier P and Patillo C, eds. (1999). *Investment and Risk in Africa*. London: Macmillan.

Cornford A (2004). Enron and internationally agreed principles for corporate governance and the financial sector. *G24 Discussion Paper* 30. Geneva: UNCTAD.

Dabee B (2002). The role of non-traditional exports in Mauritius. In Helleiner G, ed., 2002.

Das BL (2003). *The WTO and the Multilateral Trading System: Past, Present and Future*. London: Zed Books.

Das BL (2005). *The Current Negotiations in the WTO: Options, Opportunities and Risks for Developing Countries*. London: Zed Books.

Davis G and Tilton J (2002). Should developing countries reject mining? A perspective on the debate. Mimeo. Colorado School of Mines.

de Mello L (1997). Foreign direct investment in developing countries and growth: A selective survey. *Journal of Development Studies* 34 (1): 1–34.

de Mello L (1999). Foreign direct investment–led growth: Evidence from time series and panel data. *Oxford Economic Papers* 51.

Department for International Development (DFID) (2005). *Extractive Industries Transparency Initiative Source Book*. United Kingdom's International EITI Secretariat, DFID.

Dicken P (2003). *The Global Shift*. 4th ed. New York: Guilford.

Dowrick S and Golley J (2004). Trade openness and growth: Who benefits? *Oxford Review of Economic Policy* 20 (1).

Dunning J (1984). Changes in the level and structure of international production: The last 100 years. In Cassan M, ed. *The Growth of International Business*. London: Allen and Unwin.

Dutt A (1998). Direct foreign investment, transnational corporations and growth: Some empirical evidence and a North-South model. In Kozul-Wright R and Rowthorn R, eds. *Transnational Corporations and the Global Economy*. London: Macmillan.

Easterly W (2002). What did structural adjustment adjust? Mimeo. Centre for Global Development, Washington DC, August.

Economic Commission for Africa (ECA) (2004). *Assessing Regional Integration in Africa*. ECA Policy Research Report. Addis Ababa: ECA.

Economic Commission for Latin America and the Caribbean (ECLAC) (2001). *Mining in Latin America in the Late 1990s*. Santiago, Chile: ECLAC.

Economic Commission for Latin America and the Caribbean (ECLAC) (2003). *Foreign Investment in Latin America and the Caribbean*. Santiago, Chile: ECLAC.

Economic Commission for Latin America and the Caribbean (ECLAC) (2004). *Foreign Investment in Latin America and the Caribbean*. Santiago, Chile: ECLAC.

Elbadawi I and Mwega F (1997). Regional integration, trade and foreign direct investment in sub-Saharan Africa. In Iqbal Z and Kahn M, eds. *Trade Reform Investment in Sub-Saharan Africa*. Washington, DC: International Monetary Fund.

Evans P (1999). Transferable lessons? Re-examining the institutional prerequisites of East Asian economic policies. In Akyuz, ed., 2002.

Fafchamps M, Teal F and Toye J (2001). *Towards a Growth Strategy for Africa.* Oxford: Centre for the Study of African Economies.

Financial Times (2005). Comment and Analysis: Commodities. April 11.

Fischer S et al. (1998). Africa: Is this the turning point? *IMF Papers on Policy Analysis and Assessment*. Washington, DC: International Monetary Fund.

Fox P, Onorato WT and Strongman J (1998). *Assistance for Mineral Sector Development and Reform in Member Countries*. Washington, DC: World Bank.

Freeman R and Lindauer D (1999). Why not Africa? *NBER Working Paper* 6942. Cambridge, MA: National Bureau for Economic Research.

Galbraith K (2004). *The Economics of Innocent Fraud: Truth for Our Time*. Boston: Houghton Mifflin.

Gastanaga V et al. (1998). Host country reforms and FDI inflows: How much difference do they make? *World Development* 26 (7).

Gelb S and Black A (2004). Globalization in a middle income economy: FDI, production and the labour market in South Africa. In Milberg W, ed. *Labour and the Globalization of Production*. London: Palgrave.

Ghosh A (2004). Capital inflows and investment in developing countries. *ILO Employment Strategy Papers*. Geneva: ILO.

Gilroy B et al. (2001). *Multinational Enterprises, Foreign Direct Investment and Growth in Africa*. Heidelberg: Physica-Verlag.

Glass et al. (1999). Linkages, multinationals, and industrial development. Ohio State University, Department of Economics, Working Paper 99-16. Columbus, Ohio .

Gorg H and Greenaway D (2001). Foreign direct investment and intra-industry spillovers. Paper prepared for the UNECE/EBRD Expert Meeting "Financing for Development", Geneva, 3 December.

Gray HP (2004). Assessing the need for controls over inward direct investment in developing countries. *Global Economy Journal* 4 (2).

Hale D (2005). How marginal is Africa? *Resource Investor*, 25 February. *www.ResourceInvestor.com*

Hallward-Driemeier (2003). Do bilateral investment treaties attract FDI? Only a bit .... and they could bite. Mimeo. Washington, DC: World Bank.

Hanson G (2001). Should countries promote FDI? *G24 Discussion Paper Series* 9. Geneva: UNCTAD.

Harrison A (1996). Determinants and affects of direct foreign investment in Côte d'Ivoire, Morocco and Venezuela. In Roberts M and Tybout J, eds. *Industrial Evolution in Developing Countries*. Oxford: Oxford University Press.

Harrison A and McMillan M (2002). Does direct foreign investment affect domestic firms credit constraints? Mimeo. University of California, Berkeley, January.

Haslam P (2004). The bargaining gap: Explaining the stability of domestic foreign investment regimes and the limitations on state bargaining in a globalized economy. Paper presented at the eighth International Business Conference, Guadalajara, Mexico, 9 January.

Hatcher P (2004). Mali: Rewriting the Mining Code or redefining the role of the state. In Campbell, ed., 2004

Hausmann R and Fernandez-Arias E (2000). Foreign direct investment: Good cholesterol? Paper prepared for the seminar "The New Wave of Capital Flows: Sea Change or Just Another Tide?" March 26, New Orleans.

Helleiner G (1989). Transnational corporations and direct foreign investment. In Chenery H and Srinivasan TN, eds. *Handbook of Development Economics*, vol. 11. Amsterdam: Elsevier Science Publishers.

Helleiner G, ed. (2002). *Non-Traditional Export Promotion in Africa: Experience and Issues*. New York: Palgrave.

Hermes N and Lensink R (2003). Foreign direct investment, financial development and economic growth. *Journal of Development Studies* 38.

Hilson G and Potter C (2005). Structural adjustment and subsistence industry: Artisanal gold mining in Ghana. *Development and Change* 36 (1).

Hinkle L and Herrou-Aragon A (2001). How far did Africa's first generation trade reforms go? Mimeo. Washington, DC: World Bank.

Humphreys J (2003). Commodities, diversification and poverty reduction. Paper presented at FAO Symposium, Rome, 15–16 December.

International Labour Organization (ILO) (2003). *A Fair Globalization: Creating Opportunities for All*. Geneva: ILO.

International Monetary Fund (IMF) (1999). Growth in sub-Saharan Africa: Performance, impediments and policy requirements. *World Economic Outlook*, chapter VI. Washington, DC: IMF.

International Monetary Fund (IMF) (2004). *Foreign Direct Investment: Trends, Data, Availability, Concepts and Recording Practices*. Washington, DC: International Monetary Fund.

Jaunette F (2004). Foreign direct investment and regional trade agreements: The market size effect revisited. *IMF Working Paper* 206. Washington, DC: International Monetary Fund.

Johnson H (1968). *Economic Policies towards Less Developed Countries*. London: Allen and Unwin.

Jomo KS and Rock M (2003). Resource exports and resource processing for exports in Southeast Asia. In Aryeetey E et al., eds. *Asia and Africa in the Global Economy*. Tokyo: UNU Press.

Kamaly A (2003a). "Behind the surge of FDI to developing countries in the 1990s: An empirical investigation". Mimeo Department of Economics, University of Cairo, September.

Kamaly A (2003b). Mergers and acquisitions: The forgotten facet of FDI. Mimeo, Department of Economics, University of Cairo, September.

Kapur D and Webb R (2000). Governance-related conditionalities of international financial institutions. *G24 Discussion Paper Series* 6. Geneva: UNCTAD.

Karingi S, Land R, Oulmane N, Perez R, Jallab MS and Hammouda HB (2005). Economic and welfare impacts of the EU-Africa Economic Partnership Agreements. *ATPC Work in Progress* 10. Addis Ababa: African Trade Policy Centre, ECA.

Kennedy C (1991). Relations between transnational corporations and Governments of host countries: A look to the future. *Transnational Corporations*, No. 1.

Kobrin S (2005). The determinants of liberalization of FDI policy in developing countries: A cross-sectional analysis, 1992–2001. *Transnational Corporations* 14 (1).

Kozul-Wright R and Rowthorn R (2002). Globalization and the myth of economic convergence. *Economie appliqué* 55 (2).

Kregel J (1996). Some risks and implications of financial globalization for national policy autonomy, *UNCTAD Review*, Geneva.

Kregel J (2004). External financing for development and international financial stability. *G24 Discussion Paper Series* 32. Geneva: UNCTAD.

Krugman P (1995). Growing world trade: Causes and consequences. *Brookings Papers on Economic Activity* 1, Brookings Institute, Washington DC.

Krugman P (1998). Fire-sale FDI. Prepared for NBER Conference on Capital. Flows to Emerging Markets, Feb. 20–21, MIT, Cambridge, MA. Mimeo.

Kumar N and Pradhan JP (2002). Foreign direct investment, externalities and economic growth in developing countries: Some empirical explorations and implications for WTO negotiations on investment. Research and Information System for the Non-Aligned and Other Developing Countries. *RIS Discussion Paper 27*.

Kumar R (1990). Policy reform to expand mining investment in sub-Saharan Africa. *Resources Policy*, December.

Lall S (1995). Structural adjustment and African industry. *World Development* 23 (12).

Lall S (2004). Is African industry competing? *QEH Working Paper* 121. Oxford: Queen Elizabeth House.

Lensink R and Morrissey O (2002). *The Volatility of FDI, Not the Level, Affects Growth in Developing Countries*. CDS Research Report. University of Groningen, Groningen ISSN 1385-9218.

Liebenthal A, Michelitsch R and Tarazona E (2003). *Extractive Industries and Sustainable Development: An Evaluation of World Bank Group Experience*. Washington, DC: World Bank.

Lim E-G (2001). Determinants of, and relation between, foreign direct investment and growth: A summary of the recent literature. *IMF Working Paper 175*. Washington, DC: International Monetary Fund.

Lissu TA (2001). In gold we trust: The political economy of law, human rights and the environment in Tanzania's mining industry. Work in progress. *Law, Social Justice and Global Development Journal* 2. www2.warwick.ac.uk/fac/soc/law/elj/lgd/2001_2/lissu1/lissu.rtf

Lissu TA (n.d.). Globalization, national economy and the politics of Tanzania's mining industry. Extracts from Lissu, 2001Lyakurwa W (2003). Primary exports and primary processing for exports in sub-Saharan Africa. In Aryeetey E et al., eds. *Asia and Africa in the Global Economy*. Tokyo: UNU Press.

Markusen JR (1995). The boundaries of multinational enterprises and the theory of international trade. *Journal of Economic Perspectives* 9 (2).

Mate K (2002). Communities, Civil Society Organizations and the management of Mineral Wealth. Report no. 16, International Institute for Environment and Development and World Business Council for Sustainable Development, April.

McKern B (1999). Transnational corporations and the exploitation of natural resources. In UNCTAD, *Transnational Corporations and World Development*. ITB Press, London.

Mhone GCZ (2000). Enclavity and constrained labour absorptive capacity in southern African countries. *ILO/SAMAT Discussion Paper* 12. International Labour Organization Southern Africa Multidisciplinary Advisory Team, Harare, Zimbabwe.

Milanovic B (2002). Ricardian vice: Why Sala-I-Martin's calculations of world income are wrong. Mimeo. Washington, DC: World Bank.

Mining Journal (2005). 2004: A record year for mining investments. February 4.

Ministerio de Minería de Chile (2005). Punto minero 03, April.

Mkandawire T (2001). Thinking about development states in Africa. *Cambridge Journal of Economics* 25 (3).

Mkandawire T (2004). Maladjusted African economies and globalisation. Mimeo. Geneva: UNRISD.

Mody A (2004). Is FDI integrating the world economy? Paper presented at the Thirteenth World Congress of the International Economics Association, Lisbon, Portugal, September 2002. Forthcoming in *World Economy*.

Morrisett J (2000). Foreign direct investment in Africa: Policies also matter. *Transnational Corporations* 9 (2).

Moss T et al. (2004). Is Africa's scepticism at foreign capital justified? Evidence from East African firm survey data. Center for Global Development, Working Paper 41. Washington, DC.

Murshid A and Mody A (2002). Growing up with capital flows. *IMF Working Paper* 75. Washington, DC: International Monetary Fund.

Nair-Reichert U and Weinhold D (2001). Causality tests for cross-country panels: New look of FDI and economic growth in developing countries. *Oxford Bulletin of Economics and Statistics* 2.

Nayyar D (2002). Towards global governance. In Nayyar D, ed. *Governing Globalization: Issues and Institutions*. Oxford: Oxford University Press.

Ndikumana L (2003). Capital flows, capital account regimes and foreign exchange regimes in Africa. In UNCTAD, *Management of Capital Flows: Comparative Experiences and Implications for Africa*. Geneva: United Nations.

NEPAD Secretariat (2001). *"The New Partnership for Africa's Development" (NEPAD)*, October, Abuja, Nigeria.

Nunnenkamp P and Spatz J (2004). FDI and economic growth in developing countries: How relevant are host-economy and industry characteristics? *Transnational Corporations* 13 (3).

Office of Technology Assessment (OTA) (1993). *Multinationals and the National Interest*. Washington, DC: Office of Technology Assessment, US Congress.

Organisation for Economic Co-operation and Development (OECD) (2002). *Foreign Direct Investment for Development: Maximising Benefits, Minimising Costs*. Paris: OECD.

Organisation for Economic Co-operation and Development (OECD) (2003*)*. The impact of trade-related intellectual property rights on trade and foreign direct investment in developing countries. Working Party of the Trade Committee. TD/TC/WP(2002)42/ FINAL. Paris: OECD.

Ostensson O and Uwizeye-Mapendano A (2000). Growth and diversification in mineral economies. Regional workshop for mineral economies in Africa, Cape Town, South Africa, November 7–9.

Otto J, Batarseh ML and Cordes J (2000). *Global Mining Taxation Comparative Study.* 2nd ed. Institute for Global Resources Policy and Management, Colorado School of Mines, Golden, Colorado.

Owusu-Koranteng H (2004). "Environment, water and health impacts on women due to mining: The case of Wassa West and Adansi West districts of Ghana". Paper presented at the Third International Women and Mining Conference, Visakhapatnam, India, 1–9 October.

Owusu-Koranteng D (2005). Poverty, Development and Conflicts. Edberg Seminar 2005: "The Dawn of a New Era? On conflict resolution, participation and the possibilities for sustainable development".

Pigatto M (2001). The foreign direct investment environment in Africa. *Africa Region Working Paper* 15. Washington, DC: World Bank.

Piper U (2000). Deindustrialization and the social and economic sustainability nexus in developing countries: Cross-country evidence in productivity and employment. *Journal of Development Studies* 36 (4).

Plender J (2003). *Going Off the Rails: Global Capital and the Crisis of Legitimacy.* Chichester: Wiley.

Prasad E et al. (2003). Effects of financial globalization on developing countries: Some empirical evidence. *IMF Occasional Paper* 220. Washington, DC: International Monetary Fund.

Pritchett L (1996). Measuring outward orientation in LDCs: Can it be done? *Journal of Development Economics* 49.

Rasiah R (1998). The export manufacturing experience of Indonesia, Malaysia and Thailand: Lessons for Africa. *UNCTAD Discussion Paper* 137. Geneva: UNCTAD.

Reinhart C and Rogoff K (2002). FDI to Africa: The role of price stability and currency convertibility. Paper prepared for the Annual World Bank Conference on Development Economics (ABCDE) Conference, Washington, DC, April.

Rodriguez F and Rodrik D (1999). Trade policy and economic growth: A sceptic's guide to the cross-national evidence. *NBER Working Paper* 7081. Cambridge, MA: National Bureau of Economic Research.

Rodriguez-Clare A (1996). Multinationals, linkages and economic development. *American Economic Review* 86 (4).

Rodrik D (1999). *The New Global Economy and Developing Countries: Making Openness Work.* Washington, DC: Overseas Development Council.

Rodrik D (2001). Trading in illusions. *Foreign Policy*, March/April.

Rodrik D (2004). Industrial policy for the 21st century. *CEPR Discussion Paper* 4767. London: CEPR.

Ros J (2001). *Development Theory and Economic Growth.* Ann Arbor: University of Michigan Press.

Sachs J and Warner A (1995). Economic reform and the process of global integration. *Brookings Papers on Economic Activity* 1, Brookings Institute, Washington DC.

Sachs J et al. (2004). Ending Africa's poverty trap. *Brookings Papers on Economic Activity* 1, Brookings Institute, Washington DC.

Safarian E (1999). Host country policies towards inward foreign direct investment in the 1950s and the 1990s. *Transnational Corporations* 8 (2).

Sala-I-Martin X (2002). The world distribution of income. *NBER Working Paper* 8905. Cambridge, MA: National Bureau of Economic Research.

Schneider F (2002). Size and measurement of the informal economy in 110 countries around the world. Paper presented at an Australian National Tax Centre workshop, Canberra, July 17.

Sen A (1971). Methods of evaluating the economic effects of private foreign investment. UNCTAD Trade and Development Board. TD/B/C:3/94/Add.1/Corr.1. December 1.

Singh A et al. (2004). Corporate governance, competition, the new international financial architecture and large corporations in emerging markets. In UNCTAD, *Management of Capital Flows: Comparative Experiences and Implications for Africa*. Geneva: UNCTAD.

Soludo C (2003). Export-oriented industrialization and foreign direct investment in Africa. In Aryeetey E et al., *Asia and Africa in the Global Economy*. Tokyo: UNU Press.

South Africa Foundation (2004). South Africa's business presence in Africa. *Occasional Paper* 3/2004.

South Centre (1997). *Foreign Direct Investment, Development and the New Global Economic Order: A Policy Brief for the South*. Geneva: South Centre.

South Centre (2000). GATS 2000 negotiations: Options for developing countries. *Trade-Related Development and Equity (T.R.A.D.E) Working Paper* 9. Geneva: South Centre.

Spiezia V (2004). Trade, foreign direct investment and employment: Some empirical evidence. In Lee E and Vivarelli M, eds. *Understanding Globalization, Employment and Poverty Reduction*. London: Macmillan.

Stiglitz J (2002). *Globalization and Its Discontents*. New York: Norton.

Subramanian A and Roy D (2003). Who can explain the Mauritian miracle? Meade, Romer, Sachs or Rodrik? In Rodrik D, ed. *In Search of Prosperity: Analytic Narratives on Economic Growth*. Princeton: Princeton University Press.

Sutcliffe R (1998). Development: Capitalism sans frontière. *SUNS*, November 10,.

Szingare A (2004). Bringing the development state back in: Contrasting development trajectories in sub-Saharan Africa and East Asia. Paper presented to the Society for the Advancement of Socio-Economics, George Washington University, Washington, DC, 9–11 July.

Tahari A et al. (2004). Sources of growth in sub-Saharan Africa. *IMF Working Paper* 176. Washington, DC: International Monetary Fund.

Taylor I (2002). Botswana's Developmental State and the Politics of Legitimacy. Paper presented at the conference "Towards a New Political Economy of Development: Globalisation and Governance", University of Sheffield, July 4–6.

Thirlwall A (2004). The structure of production, the balance of payments and growth in developing countries. Paper presented at UNCTAD workshop, Geneva, 22 November.

Todaro M (1983). *Economic Development in the Third World*. New York: Longman.

United Nations (2005). *Investing in Development: A Practical Plan to Achieve the Millennium Development Goals. Overview*. New York: United Nations.

UNCTAD (1972). "Private Foreign Investment in Its Relationship to Development". UNCTAD III Conference, Volume III *Financing and Invisibles*, Geneva: UNCTAD.

UNCTAD (1993). *World Investment Report 1993*. United Nations publication, sales no. E.93.II.A.14. New York and Geneva.

UNCTAD (1994). *Trade and Development Report, 1994*. United Nations publication, sales no. E.94.II.D.26. New York and Geneva.

UNCTAD (1995). *Trade and Development Report, 1995*. United Nations publication, sales no. E.95.II.D.16. New York and Geneva.

UNCTAD (1996a). *The Least Developed Countries Report*. United Nations Publication, sales no. E.96.II.D.3. New York and Geneva.

UNCTAD (1996b). *Trade and Development Report, 1996*. United Nations publication, sales no. E.96.II.D.6. New York and Geneva.

UNCTAD (1997). *Trade and Development Report, 1997*. United Nations publication, sales no. E.97.II.D.8, New York and Geneva.

UNCTAD (1998). *Trade and Development Report, 1998*. United Nations publication, sales no. E.98.II.D.6, New York and Geneva.

UNCTAD (1999a). *World Investment Report 1999*. United Nations publication, sales no. E.99.II.D.3. New York and Geneva.

UNCTAD (1999b). *Trade and Development Report, 1999*. United Nations publication, sales no. E.99.II.D.1. New York and Geneva.

UNCTAD (1999c). *Foreign Direct Investment in Africa: Performance and Potential*. United Nations Publication, GE.99-52096-June 1999-5900. Geneva.

UNCTAD (1999d). Home country measures. UNCTAD/ITE/IIT/24. Geneva: UNCTAD.

UNCTAD (2000a). *World Investment Report 2000*. United Nations publication, sales no. E.00.II.D.20, New York and Geneva.

UNCTAD (2000b). *Positive Agenda and Future Trade Negotiations*. United Nations publication, sales no. E.00.II.D.8. New York and Geneva.

UNCTAD (2000c). *Capital Flows and Growth in Africa*. UNCTAD/GDS/MDPB/7. New York and Geneva: United Nations.

UNCTAD (2001a). *World Investment Report 2001*. United Nations publication, sales no. E.01.II.D.12, New York and Geneva.

UNCTAD (2001b). *Trade and Development Report, 2001*. United Nations publication, sales no. E.00.II.D.10, New York and Geneva.

UNCTAD (2002a). *World Investment Report 2002*. United Nations Publication, sales no. E.02.II.D.4, New York and Geneva.

UNCTAD (2002b). *Economic Development in Africa: From Adjustment to Poverty Reduction: What Is New?* United Nations publication, sales no. E.02.II.D.18, New York and Geneva.

UNCTAD (2002c). *The Least Developed Countries Report*. United Nations Publication, sales no. E.02.II.D.13, New York and Geneva.

UNCTAD (2002d). *Trade and Development Report, 2002*. United Nations publication, sales no. E.02.II.D.2, New York and Geneva.

UNCTAD (2003a). *Trade and Development Report, 2003*. United Nations publication, sales no. E.03.II.D.7, New York and Geneva.

UNCTAD (2003b). *Economic Development in Africa: Trade Performance and Commodity Dependence.* United Nations publication, sales no. E.03.II.D.34, New York and Geneva.

UNCTAD (2004). *World Investment Report 2004: The Shift towards Services.* United Nations Publications, sales no. E.04.II.D.36, New York and Geneva.

UNCTAD (2005a). Emerging FDI from developing countries. Note by the UNCTAD secretariat. Trade and Development Board, Commission on Investment, Technology and Related Financial Flows, 7–11 March, UNCTAD, Geneva.

UNCTAD (2005b). "Trade in services and development implications". TD/B/COM.171. Note by the UNCTAD secretariat for the Trade and Development Board, Commission on Trade in Goods, Services, and Commodities, 14–18 March, Geneva.

UNCTAD (2005c). "FDI in Africa". A note prepared by the UNCTAD secretariat for the Third African Union Conference of Ministers of Trade, 5–9 June, Cairo, Egypt.

UNCTAD (2005d). "Developments and issues in the negotiations of Economic Partnership Agreements between African ACP States and EU", TI/TMIN/EXP/8 - a (III). Note by the UNCTAD secretariat for the Third African Union Conference of Ministers of Trade, 5–9 June, Cairo, Egypt.

UNCTAD (various years). *Investment Policy Reviews.* Geneva: UNCTAD.

United Nations Industrial Development Organization (UNIDO) (2003). *African Foreign Investor Survey 2003.* Vienna: UNIDO.

United Nations Industrial Development Organization (UNIDO) (2004). *Industrial Development Report.* Vienna: UNIDO.

Van Arkadie B (1995). The state and economic change in Africa. In Chang HJ and Rowthorn R, eds. *The Role of the State in Economic Change.* Oxford: Clarendon Press.

van der Veen P (2000). The World Bank experience. Lessons from 10 years of mining sector reform: The road travelled. Paper presented at the Mining and Taxation Workshop, Washington, DC, World Bank, April 4–5.

Vora A (2001). Impact of foreign direct investment on developing country credit markets. Mimeo. University of Chicago, May.

Vreeland R (2003). *The IMF and Economic Development.* Cambridge: Cambridge University Press.

Wade R (2003). Creating capitalisms. New introduction to *Governing the Market.* Princeton: Princeton University Press.

Weatherspoon D et al. (2001). Linking globalization, economic growth and poverty: Impacts of agribusiness strategies in sub-Saharan Africa. *Staff Paper* 6, November. Department of Applied Economics and Management, Cornell University, Ithaca.

Weber-Fahr M, Strongman JE, Kunanayagam R, McMahon G and Sheldon C (2001). Mining. *PRSP Sourcebook*, Chapter 25. Washington, DC: International Monetary Fund.

Wolf M (2004). *Why Globalization Works.* New Haven: Yale University Press.

Woo-Cummings M, ed. (1999*). The Developmental State.* Ithaca: Cornell University Press.

Woodward D (2001). *The Next Crisis: Direct and Equity Investment in Developing Countries.* London: Zed Books.

World Bank (1992). *Strategy for African Mining.* World Bank Technical Paper No. 181. African Technical Department Series Mining Unit, Industry and Energy Division. Washington, DC: World Bank.

World Bank (1997). *Global Economic Prospects and the Development Countries*. Washington, DC: World Bank.

World Bank (1999). *Global Development Finance 1999: Analysis and Summary Tables*. Chapter 3. Washington, DC: World Bank.

World Bank (2000a). *Can Africa Claim the 21st Century?* Washington, DC: World Bank.

World Bank (2000b). *East Asia Recovery and Beyond*. Washington, DC: World Bank

World Bank (2001). *Global Development Finance 2001*. Washington, DC: World Bank.

World Bank (2002). *Globalization, Growth and Poverty: Building an Inclusive World Economy*. Washington, DC: World Bank.

World Bank (2003). *Project Performance Assessment Report: Ghana Mining Sector Rehabilitation Project*, Report no. 26197, Sector and Thematic Evaluation Group, OED, Washington DC: World Bank.

World Bank (2004a). *Global Development Finance: Harnessing Cyclical Gains for Development*. Washington, DC: World Bank.

World Bank (2004b). *Striking a Better Balance – The World Bank Group and the Extractive Industries: The Final Report of the Extractive Industries Review*. World Bank Management Response, 17 September. Washington, DC: World Bank.

World Bank (2005a). *Global Development Finance*, ch. 5. Washington, DC: World Bank.

World Bank (2005b). *Global Agriculture Trade and Developing Countries*. Washington, DC: World Bank.

World Bank (2005c). *2004 Annual Review of Development Effectiveness: The Bank's Contribution to Poverty Reduction*. Washington, DC: World Bank.

World Trade Organization (WTO) (1996). *World Trade Organization Annual Report 1996*. Geneva: WTO.

World Trade Organization (WTO) (2004). *The Future of the WTO: Addressing Institutional Challenges in the New Millennium*. Report by the Consultative Board to the Director-General. Geneva: WTO.

Yang Y and Gupta S (2005). Regional trading arrangements in Africa: Past performance and the way forward. *IMF Working Paper WP/05/36*. Washington, DC: International Monetary Fund.

Yashir F (1988). *Mining in Africa Today: Strategies and Prospects*. Tokyo: UNU Press.